BRITISH RAIL

LOCC

CW00376769

THIRTY-NINTH EDITION
SUMMER/AUTUMN 1997

The Complete Guide to all
Locomotives which run on
Britain's Mainline Railways

Peter Fox and Richard Bolsover

ISBN 1 872524 95 8

© 1997. Platform 5 Publishing Ltd., 3 Wyvern House, Sark Road, Sheffield,
S2 4HG, England.

CONTENTS

ACQUISITION OF INFORMATION

This book has been published with great difficulty. Privatisation of the railways and the splitting up of BR into different companies has been used as an excuse to deny the railway press access to official rolling stock library information, breaking a tradition of freely-supplied information which has existed for around half a century. We hope that readers will find the information accurate, but cannot be responsible for any inaccuracies.

We would like to thank the companies and individuals which have been co-operative in supplying information and would ask other companies which find this book useful to help us in future to make the book as accurate as possible.

This book is updated to 14th July 1997.

ORGANISATION OF BRITAIN'S RAILWAY SYSTEM

INFRASTRUCTURE

Britains state-owned railway infrastructure, i.e. the track, signalling, stations and overhead line equipment is now owned by a private company called 'Railtrack'. This has recently been privatised. Many stations and maintenance depots are leased to train operating companies. The exception is the infrastructure on the Isle of Wight, which is leased to Island Line.

DOMESTIC PASSENGER TRAIN OPERATIONS

Passenger trains are operated by train operating companies (TOCs). All TOCs have now been franchised to private operators. A list of these is appended below:

TOC	Operator	New Name
Anglia Railways	GB Trains	
Inter City East Coast	Sea Containers Ltd.	Great North Eastern Railway
Inter City West Coast	Virgin Group	Virgin Trains
Cross Country Trains	Virgin Group	Virgin Trains
Great Western Trains	Great Western Holdings	
North West Regional Railways	Great Western Holdings	North Western Trains
Midland Main Line	National Express	
Gatwick Express	National Express	
North London Railways	National Express	
Central Trains	National Express	
Scotrail	National Express	
Merseyrail Electrics	MTL Holdings	
Regional Railways North East	MTL Holdings	
LTS Rail	Prism Rail	
South Wales & West Railway	Prism Rail	
Cardiff Railway Co.	Prism Rail	
West Anglia Great Northern	Prism Rail	
South West Trains	Stagecoach	
Island Line	Stagecoach	
Network South Central	Connex	Connex South Central
South East Trains	Connex	Connex South Eastern
Great Eastern	FirstBus	
Thameslink	GOVIA	
Chiltern Railways	M40 Trains	
Thames Trains	Victory Rail	

NOTES ON TRAIN OPERATING COMPANY OWNERS

Connex

This is a French company owned by Société Générale des Entreprises Automobiles, a subsidiary of Compagnie Générale des Eaux.

FirstBus

This is a large bus company which was originally formed by the amalgamation of Badgerline and GRT bus group.

GB Trains

This is a company set up for rail privatisation.

GOVIA

A joint venture between the Go-Ahead bus company and VIA, a French public transport operating company.

Great Western Holdings

This is a jointly owned by the former Great Western Trains management. 3i plc and FirstBus.

National Express

This is a transport operator which runs express coach services by sub-contracting them to various bus companies. It also owns east Midlands Airport.

M40 Trains

This is owned by the former management of Chiltern Railways.

MTL Holdings

This is the former municipal bus operator Merseyside PTE which operates buses in Merseyside and London.

Prism

This is a company whose shares are owned by individuals and financial institutions. Its chairman is joint managing director of EYMS, a bus company.

Sea Containers

This is a Bermuda-based shipping company which also owns the Venice-Simplon-Orient Express.

Stagecoach

Tha largest private bus operator in the UK.

Victory Railway Holdings

This is a joint venture between the Go Ahead group and Thames Trains managament.

Virgin Group

This is the well-known company headed by Richard Branson which has interests in travel, leisure and retailing.

CHANNEL TUNNEL PASSENGER TRAIN OPERATIONS

Eurostar trains are operated by Eurostar (UK) Ltd. jointly with French Railways (SNCF) and Belgian Railways (NMBS/SNCB). Eurostar (UK) will also operate the Night Service trains jointly with SNCF, Netherlands Railways (NS) and German Railways (DB).

FREIGHT TRAIN OPERATIONS

The three trainload freight companies Loadhaul, Mainline and Transrail which were set up on the government's orders in readiness for privatisation have been sold to the North & South Railway Company whose main shareholder is Wisconsin Central Transportation Corporation of the USA. Rail Express Systems, which operates mail and charter trains has also been sold to this company. The four concerns have been combined and now known as the English, Welsh and Scottish Railway Ltd. (EWS). Railfreight Distribution (RfD) which operates general freight, particularly Channel Tunnel traffic, is also to be sold to EWS but the sale has been held up by the European Union.

The container train operation known as Freightliner has been sold to a managament buyout known as Freightliner (1995) Ltd.

Certain other companies e.g. Direct Rail Services and National Power operate freight trains with their own locomotives.

OWNERSHIP OF LOCOMOTIVES AND ROLLING STOCK

The locomotives of EWS and those of Eurostar are owned by those companies. Most locomotives, hauled coaching stock and multiple unit vehicles used by the passenger train operating companies are owned by three leasing companies which were originally set up by British Railways as subsidiaries and then privatised. These are Eversholt Holdings (formerly Eversholt Leasing), Angel Train Contracts and Porterbrook Leasing Company Ltd.

Other vehicles are owned by various private companies such as Fragonset Railways, Carnforth Railway Restoration & Engineering Services Ltd., Titanstar Ltd. and the Venice-Simplon-Orient Express Ltd.

Further details of these companies will be found in the section on abbreviations and codes. Thus for each vehicle it is generally necessary to specify both the owner and the TOC which currently operates the vehicle.

A number of 'service' type vehicles are owned by Railtrack (e.g. Sandite vehicles) and others are owned by former BR Headquarters organisations which have now been privatised e.g. Railtest or by railway vehicle manufacturing and repair companies. Royal Train vehicles are owned by Railtrack.

In this book, where the owner is different to the operator given in the pool code, the owning company is detailed in the information section at the head of each class.

INTRODUCTION

The following notes are applicable to locomotives:

DETAILS & DIMENSIONS

Principal details and dimensions are given for each class in metric units. Imperial equivalents are also given for power. Maximum speeds are still quoted in miles per hour since imperial units are still used in day to day railway operations in Britain.. Since the present maximum permissible speed of certain classes of locomotives is different from the design speed, these are now shown separately in class details. In some cases certain low speed limits are arbitrary and may occasionally be raised when necessary if a locomotive has to be pressed into passenger service.

LOCOMOTIVE DETAIL DIFFERENCES

Detail differences which affect the areas and types of train which locos work are shown. Where detail differences occur within a class or part class of locomotives., these are shown against the individual locomotive number. Except where shown, diesel locomotives have no train heating equipment. Electric or electro-diesel locomotives are assumed to have train heating unless shown otherwise. Standard abbreviations used are:

a   Train air brakes only.
c   Fitted with Scharfenberg couplers for Eurostar working.
e   Fitted with electric heating apparatus (ETH).
j   Fitted with RCH jumper cables for operating with PCVs (propelling control vehicles).
r   Fitted with radio electronic token block equipment.
s   Slow speed control fitted (and operable).
t   Fitted with automatic vehicle identification transponders.
v   Train vacuum brakes only.
x   Dual train brakes (air & vacuum).
y   ETH equipped but equipment isolated.
+   Extended range locos with Additional fuel tank capacity compared with others in class.

After the locomotive number are shown any notes regarding braking, heating etc., the livery code (in bold type), the pool code where applicable, the depot code and name if any. Locomotives which have been renumbered in recent years show the last number in parentheses after the current number. For previous numbers of other locos, please refer to the Platform 5 Book 'Diesel & Electric Loco Register'.

NAMES

All official names are shown as they appear on the locomotive i.e. all upper case or upper & lower case lettering. Where only a few locomotives in a class are named, these are shown in a separate table at the end of the class or sub-class.

DEPOT ALLOCATIONS & POOL CODES

The depot at which a locomotive is allocated is the one at which it receives its main examinations. This depot may be a long way away from where it normally performs its duties. The pool code is a better means of ascertaining where a locomotive may operate, but it should be borne in mind that often locomotives of the same company may be used in pools other than their official pool.In addition, English Welsh & Scottish Railway are likely to move towards a common user system in future. (S) denotes stored serviceable and (U) stored unserviceable. Locos may not be stored at their home depots. Thus the layout is as follows:

No.	Old No.	Notes	Livery	Pool	Depot	Name
47777	(47636)	**RX**		PXLB	CD	Restored

GENERAL INFORMATION ON BRITISH RAILWAYS' LOCOMOTIVES

CLASSIFICATION & NUMBERING

Initially BR diesel locomotives were allocated numbers in the 1xxxx series, with electrics allotted numbers in the 2xxxx series. Around 1957 diesel locomotives were allocated new numbers with between one and four digits with 'D' prefixes. Diesel electric shunters in the 13xxx series had the '1' replaced by a 'D', but diesel mechanical shunters were completely renumbered. Electric locomotives retained their previous numbers but with an 'E' prefix.

When all standard gauge steam locomotives had been withdrawn, the prefix letter was removed. In 1972, the present TOPS numbering system was introduced whereby the loco number consisted of a two-digit class number followed by a serial number. In some cases the last two digits of the former number were generally retained (Classes 20, 37, 50), but in other classes this is not the case. In this book former TOPS numbers carried byrecently- converted locos. are shown in parentheses. Full renumbering information is to be found in the 'Diesel & Electric loco Register', the new third edition of which is now available.

Diesel locomotives are classified as 'types' depending on their engine horsepower as follows:

Type	Engine hp.	Old Number Range	Current Classes
1	800-1000	D 8000-D 8999	20.
2	1001-1499	D 5000-D 6499/D 7500-D 7999	31.
3	1500-1999	D 6500-D 7499	33, 37.
4	2000-2999	D 1-D 1999	46, 47.
5	3000+	D 9000-D 9499	55, 56, 58, 59, 60.
Shunter	300-799	D 3000-D 4999	08, 09.

Class 14 (650 hp diesel hydraulics) were numbered in the D95xx series.

Electric and electro-diesel locomotives are classified according to their supply system. Locomotives operating on a d.c. system are allocated classes 71-80, whilst a.c. or dual voltage locomotives start at Class 81. Departmental locomotives which remain self propelled or which are likely to move around on a day to day basis are classified Class 97.

WHEEL ARRANGEMENT

For main line diesel and electric locomotives the system whereby the number of driven axles on a bogie or frame is denoted by a letter (A=1, B=2, C=3 etc.) and the number of undriven axles is noted by a number is used. The letter 'o' after a letter indicates that each axle is individually powered and a + sign indicates that the bogies are intercoupled. For shunters the Whyte notation is used. In this notation, generally used in Britain for steam locomotives, the number of leading wheels are given, followed by the number of driving wheels and then the trailing wheels.

HAULING CAPABILITY OF DIESEL LOCOS

The hauling capability of a diesel locomotive depends basically upon three factors:

1. Its adhesive weight. The greater the weight on its driving wheels, the greater the adhesion and thus more tractive power can be applied before wheel slip occurs.

2. The characteristics of its transmission. In order to start a train the locomotive has to exert a pull at standstill. A direct drive diesel engine cannot do this, hence the need for transmission. This may be mechanical, hydraulic or electric. The current British standard for locomotives is electric transmission. Here the diesel engine drives a generator or alternator and the current produced is fed to the traction motors. The force produced by each driven wheel depends on the current in its traction motor. In other words the larger the current, the harder it pulls.

As the locomotive speed increases, the current in the traction motors falls hence the *Maximum Tractive Effort* is the maximum force at its wheels that the locomotive can exert at a standstill. The electrical equipment cannot take such high currents for long without overheating. Hence the *Continuous Tractive Effort* is quoted which represents the current which the equipment can take continuously.

3. The power of its engine. Not all of this power reaches the rail as electrical machines are approximately 90% efficient. As the electrical energy passes through two such machines (the generator/alternator and the traction motors), the *Power At Rail* is about 81% (90% of 90%) of the engine power, less a further amount used for auxiliary equipment such as radiator fans, traction motor cooling fans, air compressors, battery charging, cab heating, ETH, etc. The power of the locomotive is proportional to the tractive effort times the speed. Hence when on full power there is a speed corresponding to the continuous tractive effort.

HAULING CAPABILITY OF ELECTRIC LOCOS

Unlike a diesel locomotive, an electric locomotive does not develop its power on board and its performance is determined only by two factors, namely its weight and the characteristics of its electrical equipment. Whereas a diesel locomotive tends to be a constant power machine, the power of an electric loco-motive varies considerably. Up to a certain speed it can produce virtually a constant tractive effort. Hence power rises with speed according to the formula given in section 3 above, until a maximum speed is reached at which tractive effort falls, such that the power also falls. Hence the power at the speed corresponding to the maximum tractive effort is lower than the maximum.

BRAKE FORCE

The brake force is a measure of the braking power of a locomotive. This is shown on the locomotive data panels so that railway staff can ensure that sufficient brake power is available on freight trains.

TRAIN HEATING AND POWER EQUIPMENT

The standard system in use in Britain for heating loco hauled trains is by means of electricity and is now known as ETS (Electric train supply). Locomotives which were equipped to provide steam heating have had this equipment removed or rendered inoperable (isolated). Electric heat is provided from the locomotive by means of a separate alternator on the loco, except in the case of Class 33 which have a d.c. generator. The ETH Index is a measure of the electrical power available for train heating. All electrically heated coaches have an ETH index and the total of these in a train must not exceed the ETH power of a locomotive.

ROUTE AVAILABILITY

This is a measure of a railway vehicle's axle load. The higher the axle load of a vehicle, the higher the RA number on a scale 1 to 10. Each route on BR has an RA number and in theory no vehicle with a higher RA number may travel on that route without special clearance. Exceptions are made, however.

MULTIPLE AND PUSH-PULL WORKING

Multiple working between diesel locomotives in Britain has usually been provided by means of an electro-pneumatic system, with special jumper cables connecting the locos. A coloured symbol is painted on the end of the locomotive to denote which system is in use. Class 47s nos. 47701-17 used a time-division multiplex (t.d.m.) system which utilised the existing RCH (an abbreviation for the former railway clearing house, a pre-nationalisation standards organisation) jumper cables for push-pull working. These had in the past only been used for train lighting control, and more recently for public address (pa) and driver-guard communication. A new standard t.d.m. system is now fitted to all a.c. electric locomotives and other vehicles, enabling them to work in both push-pull and multiple working modes.

COMMUNICATION

Virtually all main line locomotives are now fitted with cab to shore radio communication. Where locomotives are fitted with train communication this is stated in the class headings.

1. DIESEL LOCOMOTIVES

CLASS 08   BR SHUNTER   0-6-0

Built: 1953–62 by BR at Crewe, Darlington, Derby, Doncaster or Horwich Works.
Engine: English Electric 6KT of 298 kW (400 hp) at 680 rpm.
Main Generator: English Electric 801.
Traction Motors: Two English Electric 506.
Max. Tractive Effort: 156 kN (35000 lbf).
Cont. Tractive Effort: 49 kN (11100 lbf) at 8.8 m.p.h.
Power At Rail: 194 kW (260 hp).   **Length over Buffers:** 8.92 m.
Brake Force: 19 t.   **Wheel Diameter:** 1372 mm.
Design Speed: 20 m.p.h.   **Weight:** 50 t.
Max. Speed: 15 or 20* m.p.h.   **RA:** 5.

Ownership:
08296/527/73/602/82/92/9/823/46/943 are owned by ADtranz.
08484/568/629/730 are owned by Railcare Ltd.
08649/847 are owned by Wessex Traincare Ltd.
Great North Eastern Railway locos Nos. 08331/892 are owned by RFS.

Non-standard liveries:
08077 is RFS grey with blue and yellow bodyside stripes.
08296, 08602, 08846 & 08943 are grey and carry numbers 001, D 3769, D 4144
and 002 respectively.
08414 is D with RfD brandings and also carries its former number D 3529.
08460 is light grey with a dark grey roof, black cab doors and window surrounds and 'TLF South East' branding.
08500 is red lined out in black & white.
08519 is BR black.
08527 is light grey with a black roof, blue bodyside stripe and 'Ilford Level 5'
branding.
08593 is Great Eastern blue lined out in red and also carries its former number
D 3760.
08601 is London Midland & Scottish Railway black.
08629 is Royal purple.
08642 is London & South Western Railway black and also carries its former
number D 3809.
08689 is D with Railfreight general markings.
08715 is in experimental dayglo orange livery.
08721 is blue with a red & yellow stripe ('Red Star' livery).
08730 is BR black.
08805 is LMS maroon and also carries its former number 3973.
08867 is BR black.
08879 is turquoise with full yellow ends, black cab doors, black numbers on a
yellow background and RfD brandings.
08883 is Caledonian blue.
08907 is London & North Western Railway black.
08938 is grey and red.

08616 carries its former number D 3783.
08830 is on long-term lease to the East Somerset Railway and carries its former number D 3998.
n Waterproofed for working at Oxley Carriage Depot.
z Fitted with buckeye adaptor at nose end for HST depot shunting.

Formerly numbered in series 3000–4192.

Class 08/0. Standard Design.

Number						Number					
08077	a	0	DFLS	EH		08511	a		FDSD	DR	
08296	x	0		ZC		08512	a	F	FDSD	DR	
08331	x	GN	HBSH	EC		08514	a		FDSD	DR	
08388	a	FP	FDSX	IM(U)		08516	a	D	ENSN	TO	
08389	a		DAWE	AN		08517	a		EWSX	SF(U)	
08393	a	D	DAYX	AN(U)		08519	a	0	LCWX	BS(U)	
08397	a	F	LWSP	CD		08523	x	ML	EWOC	OC	
08401	a		FDSI	IM		08525	x	F	HISL	NL	
08402	a	D	LWSP	CD		08526	x		EWOC	OC	
08405	a	D	FDSI	IM		08527	x	0		ZI	
08410	a	D	HJXX	PM		08528	x	D	ENSN	TO	
08411	a		LGML	ML		08529	x		ENSN	TO	
08413	a	D	DAYX	TI(U)		08530	x	D	DFLS	SF	
08414	a*	0	EWSX	OC(U) **OK**		08531	x	D	DFLS	SF	
08417	a		CDJD	DY		08534	x	D	LGML	ML	
08418	a	F	FDSD	DR		08535	x	D	DASY	TI	
08428	a		LCWX	BS(U)		08536	x		HISE	DY	
08441	a		ENSN	TO		08538	x	D	ENSN	TO	
08442	a	F	FDSK	KY		08540	x	D	ENZX	TO(U)	
08445	a		FDSX	IM(U)		08541	x	D	EWSF	SF	
08448	a		LCXX	BS(U)		08542	x	F	LBBS	BS	
08449	a		ENXX	TO(U)		08543	x	D	LBBS	BS	
08451	x		HFSN	WN		08561	x		LGML	ML	
08454	x		HFSN	WN		08567	x		ENSN	TO	
08460	a	0	EWSX	OC(U) **OK**		08568	x			ZH	
08466	a	FO	FDSX	IM(U)		08569	x		DAAN	AN	
08472	a		HBSH	BN		08571	xz		HBSH	EC	
08480	a	G	EWEH	EH		08573	x			ZI	
08481	x		LNCF	CF		08575	x	BS	DFLS	TI	
08482	a	D	DAWE	AN		08576	x		LNCF	CF	
08483	a	D	HJXX	PM		08577	x		FMSY	TE	
08484	a	D		ZN		08578	x	R	PXLS	HT	
08485	a		LWSP	CD		08580	x		ENSN	TO	
08489	a	F	LWSP	CD		08581	x	BS	FDSX	DR(U) **SCRAP**	
08492	a		ENSN	TO		08582	a	D	FMSY	TE	
08493	a		LNCF	CF		08585	x		DFLS	CD	
08495	x		ENSN	TO		08586	a	F	LCXX	AY(U)	
08499	a	F	FDSK	KY		08587	x		FDSD	DR	
08500	x	0	FDSD	DR		08588	xz	BS	HISL	NL	
08506	a		LGML	ML		08593	x	0	EWSF	SF	
08509	a	F	FDSD	DR		08594	x		PXXA	TO(U) **SCRAP**	
08510	a		FDSD	DR		08597	x		FDSK	KY	

(handwritten annotation at right: bracket spanning 08527–08543 labelled "110 VOLTS")

08599	x		PXXA	SP(U)		08697	x	HISE	DY
08600	a	D	EWEH	EH *SOLD*		08698	a	EWSU	SU
08601	x	0	LBBS	BS		08699	x	D	ZC
08602	x	0		ZD		08700	a	EWSX	SF(U) *SCRA*
08605	x		FDSK	KY		08701	x	RX	PXLS	CD
08607	x		ENXX	TO(U) *SCRA*		08702	x	PXLS	OC
08610	x		LCXX	BS(U)		08703	a	DAYX	AN(U)
08611	x		HFSL	LO		08706	x	FDSK	KY
08616	x	G	HGSS	TS		08709	x	EWOC	OC
08617	x		HFSN	WN		08711	x	RX	EWSF	SF
08619	x		LCXX	LO(U)		08713	x	FDSX	DR(U) *SCRAF*
08622	x		LCWX	ML(U)		08714	x	RX	ENSN	TO
08623	x		LBBS	BS		08715	v	0	EWSX	SF(U)
08624	x		DFLS	ML		08718	x	LCXX	AY(U)
08625	x		LCXX	CF(U) *SCRA*		08720	a	D	LGML	ML
08628	x		LBBS	BS		08721	x	0	HFSL	LO
08629	x	0		ZN		08723	x	ENXX	TO(U) *SCRAP*
08630	x		LGML	ML		08724	x	HBSH	ZB(U)
08632	x		FDSI	IM		08730	x	0		ZH
08633	x	RX	PXLS	HT		08731	x	LCWX	ML(U)
08635	x		PXLS	OC		08734	x	LCWX	CF(U)
08641	xz	D	HJSL	LA		08735	x	LGML	ML
08642	x*	0	DFLS	EH		08737	x	FE	DAWE	AN
08643	x*	D	HJXX	PM		08738	x	D	LGML	ML
08644	xz	M	HJSL	LA		08739	x	DAAN	AN
08645	x	D	HJSL	LA		08740	x	F	EWSX	SF(U)
08646	x	F	EWOC	OC		08742	x	RX	PXLS	CD
08648	x*	D	HJSL	LA		08745	x	FE	DFLS	SF
08649	x	0		ZG	*110*	08746	x	D	LBBS	BS
08651	xz	D	EWOC	OC *110 vol*		08749	x	EWSF	SF
08653	x*	FE	DAAN	AN *vol*		08751	x	FE	DAYX	TI(U)
08655	x*	F	DAYX	AN(U)		08752	x	C	EWSF	SF
08661	a	FE	DAYX	AN(U)		08754	x	HASS	IS
08662	x		FDSK	KY		08756	x	D	LNCF	CF
08663	x	D	HJSL	LA		08757	x	RX	PXLS	HT
08664	x		EWOC	OC		08758	x	EWSX	SF(U)
08665	x		FDSI	IM		08762	x	HASS	IS
08670	a		EWSX	SF(U) *OK*		08765	xn	D	LBBS	BS
08675	x	F	LGML	ML		08768	x	LGML	ML
08676	x		LWSP	CD		08770	a	D	LNCF	CF
08682	x			ZF		08773	x	ENXX	TO(U)
08683	x		LCXX	CF(U)		08775	x	EWSF	SF
08685	x		LGML	ML		08776	a	D	FDSK	KY
08689	x	0	EWSX	OC(U)		08780	x	HJSE	LE
08690	x		HISE	DY		08782	a	FDSK	KY
08691	x	G	DFLS	CD		08783	x	FDSK	KY
08692	x	0		ZC(U)		08784	x	DAYX	CE(U)
08693	x		LCWX	ML(U)		08786	a	D	LNCF	CF
08694	x		DAWE	AN		08790	x	HFSL	LO
08695	x		LWSP	CD		08792	x	LNCF	CF
08696	a	D	HFSN	WN		08795	x	M	HJSE	LE

ID				
08798	x		LNCF	CF
08799	x		DAAN	AN
08801	x		LNCF	CF
08802	x	RX	PXLS	CD
08804	x		PXLS	BK
08805	x	0	HGSS	TS
08806	a	F	FMSY	TE
08807	a	BS	LBBS	BS
08810	a		HSSN	NC
08811	a*		EWSX	OC(U)
08813	x	D	FMSY	TE
08815	x		LCWX	SP(U)
08817	x	BS	LWSP	CD
08819	x	D	LNCF	CF
08822	x	M	HJSE	LE
08823	a			ZF
08824	a	F	FDSI	IM
08825	a		DAWE	AN
08826	a		LCWX	ML(U)
08827	a		LGML	ML
08828	a	E	LNCF	CF
08830	x*	G	HLSV	CO
08834	x	FD	HBSH	BN
08836	x	I	HJXX	OO
08837	x*	D	DAAN	AN
08842	x		DAYX	AN(U)
08844	x		DAWE	AN
08846	x	0		ZC
08847	x*			ZG
08853	xr		HBSH	BN
08854	x*		EWEH	EH
08856	x		DAAN	AN
08865	x		ENSN	TO
08866	x		EWSF	SF
08867	x	0	LWSP	CD
08869	x	G	HSSN	NC
08872	x	D	DAWE	AN
08873	x	RX	PXLS	CD
08877	x	D	FDSD	DR
08878	x		EWSX	OC(U)
08879	x	0	DATI	TI
08881	x	D	LGML	ML
08882	x		LGML	ML
08883	x	0	LGML	ML
08884	x		LWSP	CD
08886	x	E	ENSN	TO
08887	x		HFSN	WN
08888	x	E	FDSI	IM
08890	x	D	PXLS	OC
08891	x		DFLS	AN
08892	x*	GN	HBSH	BN
08893	x	D	LCXX	BS(U)
08894	x		LWSP	CD
08896	x		PXLS	BK(U)
08897	x	D	PXLS	BK
08899	x		HISE	DY
08900	x	D	LNWK	CF
08901	xn		LCXX	BS(U)
08902	x		DAYX	AN(U)
08904	x		EWOC	OC
08905	x	FE	DAYX	TI(U)
08906	x		LGML	ML
08907	x	0	DAAN	AN
08908	xz		HISL	NL
08909	x		EWSF	SF
08910	x		LGML	ML
08911	x	D	LCXX	ZC(U)
08912	x	BS	LGML	ML
08913	x	D	DAYX	AN(U)
08914	x		LCXX	BS(U)
08915	x	F	LWSP	CD
08917	x	D	LWSP	CD
08918	x	RX	PXLS	BK
08919	x	F	LBBS	BS
08920	x	E	PXLS	CD
08922	x	D	LGML	ML
08924	x	D	EWOC	OC
08925	x		LWSP	CD
08926	x		DAYX	AN(U)
08927	x		LBBS	BS
08928	x	FR	HSSN	NC
08931	x		FDSX	TE(U)
08932	x		LNWK	CF
08933	x*	E	EWEH	EH
08934	x		HFSN	WN
08938	xr	0	LCWX	ML(U)
08939	x		DAAN	AN
08940	x		EWEH	EH
08941	x		LNCF	CF
08942	x		LNWK	CF
08943	x	0		ZT
08944	x	D	EWOC	OC
08946	x	FE	DASY	TI
08947	x		EWOC	OC
08948	xc	EP	GPSS	OC
08950	x	I	HISL	NL
08951	x	D	DASY	TI
08952	x		LCWX	ML(U)
08953	x	D	LNCF	CF
08954	x	FT	LNWK	CF
08955	x		LNWK	CF
08956	x		CDJD	DY

(Handwritten annotations: "CD OK" by 08897; "BS" and "O" by 08908–08910; "ZC(U) OK" by 08911; vertical notes "ALL 110 VoLTS" and "110 VoLTS".)

| 08957 | x | **E** | LNCF | CF | | 08958 | x | | EWSX | SF(U) |

Names:

08578	Libert Dickinson		08790	M.A. SMITH
08649	G.H. Stratton		08869	The Canary
08661	Europa		08879	Sheffield Children's Hospital
08682	Lionheart		08888	Postman's Pride
08701	The Sorter		08919	Steep Holm
08711	EAGLE C.U.R.C.		08950	Neville Hill 1st
08714	Cambridge			

Class 08/9. Fitted with cut-down cab and headlight for Cwmmawr branch.

08993	x	**FT**	LNWK	CF	ASHBURNHAM
08994	a	**D**	LNWK	CF	GWENDRAETH
08995	a	**FT**	LNWK	CF	KIDWELLY

CLASS 09   BR SHUNTER   0–6–0

Built: 1959–62 by BR at Darlington or Horwich Works.
Engine: English Electric 6KT of 298 kW (400 hp) at 680 rpm.
Main Generator: English Electric 801.
Traction Motors: English Electric 506.
Max. Tractive Effort: 111 kN (25000 lbf).
Cont. Tractive Effort: 39 kN (8800 lbf) at 11.6 m.p.h.
Power At Rail: 201 kW (269 hp).
Brake Force: 19 t.   **Length over Buffers:** 8.92 m.
Weight: 50 t.   **Wheel Diameter:** 1372 mm.
Max. Speed: 27 m.p.h.   **RA:** 5.
Train Brakes: Air & Vacuum.

Class 09/0 were originally numbered 3665–71, 3719–21, 4099–4114.

Class 09/0. Built as Class 09.

09001		LNCF	CF		09014	**D**	FDSK	KY
09003		EWHG	SL CF		09015	**D**	LNCF	CF
09004		HWSU	SU		09016	**D**	EWOC	OC
09005	**D**	FMSY	TE		09018	**ML**	EWOC	OC
09006	**ML**	EWOC	OC		09019	**ML**	EWHG	SL
09007	**ML**	EWOC	OC		09020		EWOC	OC
09008	**D**	LNCF	CF		09021	**FE**	DAWE	AN
09009	**E**	EWHG	SL		09022		DAYX	AN(U)
09010	**D**	EWSF	SF		09023		EWSU	SU
09011	**D**	DASY	TI		09024	**ML**	EWHG	SL
09012	**D**	EWOC	OC		09025		HWSU	SU
09013	**D**	LNCF	CF		09026	**D**	HWSU	SU

Names:

09009	Three Bridges C.E.D.	09026	William Pearson
09012	Dick Hardy		

Class 09/1. Converted from Class 08. 110 V electrical equipment.

09101	**D**	EWOC	OC
09102	**D**	EWOC	OC
09103	**D**	LGML	ML
09104	**D**	LBBS	BS
09105	**D**	LNCF	CF
09106	**D**	FMSY	TE
09107	**D**	LNCF	CF

Class 09/2. Converted from Class 08. 90 V electrical equipment.

09201	**D**	ENSN	TO
09202	**D**	LGML	ML
09203	**D**	LNCF	CF
09204	**D**	FMSY	TE
09205	**D**	LGML	ML

CLASS 20   ENGLISH ELECTRIC TYPE 1   Bo–Bo

Built: 1957–68 by English Electric Company at Vulcan Foundry, Newton le Willows or Robert Stephenson & Hawthorn, Darlington. 20001–128 were originally built with disc indicators whilst 20129–228 were built with four character headcode panels.
Engine: English Electric 8SVT Mk. II of 746 kW (1000 hp) at 850 rpm.
Main Generator: English Electric 819/3C.
Traction Motors: English Electric 526/5D (20001–48) or 526/8D (others).
Max. Tractive Effort: 187 kN (42000 lbf).
Cont. Tractive Effort: 111 kN (25000 lbf) at 11 m.p.h.
Power At Rail: 574 kW (770 hp).   **Length over Buffers:** 14.25 m.
Brake Force: 35 t.   **Wheel Diameter:** 1092 mm.
Design Speed: 75 m.p.h.   **Weight:** 73.5 t.
Max. Speed: 60 m.p.h.   **RA:** 5.
Train Brakes: Air & Vacuum.
Multiple Working: Blue Star Coupling Code. (Class 20/3 have non-standard jumpers).

Ownership:
20007/32/72/5/104/17/21/8/31/87/90/215 have recently been sold to Direct Rail Services (DRS) but no pool code change has yet been made. 20102/8/133 are also owned by DRS and are currently stored, pending possible reinstatement, at the Midland Railway Centre, Swanwick Junction (code SK).

Non-standard livery:
20102, 20108 & 20133 are RFS grey with blue and yellow bodyside stripes and carry numbers 2008, 2001 and 2005 respectively.

Originally numbered in series 8007–8190, 8315–8325.

Class 20/0. Standard Design.

20007	st		ZB (U)
20016	st	LCXX	BS (U)
20032	s		ZB (U)

20057	st		LCXX	BS (U)
20059	st	**FR**	LCXX	BS (U)
20066			LCXX	BS (U)
20072	st			ZB (U)
20075	st	**T**		SD (U)
20081	st		LCXX	BS (U)
20087	st	**BS**	LCXX	BS (U)
20092		**CS**	LCXX	BS (U)
20102		**0**		SK (U)
20104	st	**FR**		ZB (U)
20108		**0**		SK (U)
20117	st			ZB (U)
20118		**FR**	LCWX	BS (U)
20121	st			ZB (U)
20128	st	**T**		ZB (U)
20131	st	**T**		ZB (U)
20132	st	**FR**	LCWX	BS (U)
20133		**0**		SK (U)
20138		**FR**	LCWX	BS (U)
20165		**FR**	LCWX	BS (U)
20168	st		LCWX	BS (U)
20169	st	**CS**	LCWX	BS (U)
20187	st	**T**		SD (U)
20190	st			ZB (U)
20215	st	**FR**		ZB (U)

Class 20/3. Privately-owned by Direct Rail Services.
Used on radioactive waste, chemical and milk trains etc.
All have train air brakes only and twin fuel tanks.

Non-standard livery:
Dark blue with light blue roof and green lettering.

20301	(20047)	**0**	XHSD	SD	FURNESS RAILWAY 150
20302	(20084)	**0**	XHSD	SD	
20303	(20127)	**0**	XHSD	SD	
20304	(20120)	**0**	XHSD	SD	
20305	(20095)	**0**	XHSD	SD	

Class 20/9. Privately-owned by Hunslet–Barclay Ltd.
Used mainly on weedkilling trains.
Train air-brakes only.

Non-standard livery:
Hunslet–Barclay two-tone grey with red solebars and black lettering.

20901	t	**0**	XYPD	ZK	NANCY
20902		**0**	XYPD	ZK	LORNA
20903		**0**	XYPD	ZK	ALISON
20904		**0**	XYPD	ZK	JANIS
20905	t	**0**	XYPD	ZK	IONA
20906		**0**	XYPD	ZK	Kilmarnock 400

▲ Soon after being outshopped following an overhaul, Great North Eastern Railway liveried Class 08 No. 08892 stands in the yard of RFS at Doncaster on 2nd April 1997. **Gavin Morrison**

▼ Mainline blue liveried Class 09 No. 09018 is pictured between duties at Old Oak Common TMD on 17th August 1996. **Kevin Conkey**

▲ Direct Rail Services liveried Class 20 No. 20301 'FURNESS RAILWAY 150' is pictured coupled to another locomotive of its sub-class at Barrow Docks on 19th September 1996. **Dave McAlone**

▼ Class 20/9s have now begun their yearly tour of the network with weed-killing trains. Here, No. 20902 'LORNA' is pictured stabled between duties at Reading in May of this year. Hunslet-Barclay two-tone grey is standard for this sub-class.
Darren Ford

One of the few remaining BR blue liveried locomotives still in traffic, Class 31 No. 31450 is pictured with Civil-link liveried classmate No. 31229 at Worcester Yard on 15th September 1996.

Stephen Widdowson

Civil-link liveried Class 33s Nos. 33026 & 33019 pass Earlswood on 2nd April 1997 with 6Y94, the 09.36 Purley–Salfords Cliffe Brett stone empties.

David Brown

One of the many North Wales coast loco-hauled services, the 10.23 Bangor-Crewe is pictured passing Llanfairfechan, near Bangor behind Regional Railways liveried Class 37 No. 37414 'Cathays C&W Works 1846–1993' on 8th June 1996.

Nic Joynson

▲ Class 37 No. 37065 arrives at Hoo Junction with a Grain–Hoo trip ballast working on 22nd April 1997. This loco carries the now defunct Mainline Freight livery.   **Rodney Lissenden**

▼ Midland Mainline liveried Class 43 No. 43059 is seen at Great Bowden on 10th February 1997 whilst leading the 14.15 London St Pancras–Sheffield.

Bob Sweet

Great Western Trains liveried Class 43 No. 43137 'Newton Abbot 150' leads a similarly liveried set forming the 12.47 Newton Abbot–Penzance ECS at Silveton on 11th April 1997.
Colin Marsden

Class 47 No. 47782, in Rail express systems livery, skirts the sea wall at Dawlish on 10th April 1997 whilst returning the Royal train from Totnes to Railcare Wolverton.

Colin Marsden

CLASS 31   BRUSH TYPE 2   A1A–A1A

Built: 1957–62 by Brush Traction at Loughborough. 31102/6/7/10/25/34/44/444/50/61 retain two headcode lights. Others have roof-mounted headcode boxes.
Engine: English Electric 12SVT of 1100 kW (1470 hp) at 850 rpm.
Main Generator: Brush TG160-48.
Traction Motors: Brush TM73-68.
Max. Tractive Effort: 160 kN (35900 lbf) (190 kN (42800 lbf)*).
Cont. Tractive Effort: 83 kN (18700 lbf) at 23.5 m.p.h. (99 kN (22250 lbf) at 19.7 m.p.h. *.)

Power At Rail: 872 kW (1170 hp).	**Length over Buffers:** 17.30 m.
Brake Force: 49 t.	**Driving Wheel Diameter:** 1092 mm.
Design Speed: 90 (80*) m.p.h.	**Centre Wheel Diameter:** 1003 mm.
Weight: 107–111 t.	**Train Brakes:** Air & Vacuum.
RA: 5 or 6.	**ETH Index (Class 31/4):** 66.

Max. Speed: 60 m.p.h. (90 m.p.h. Class 31/4).
Multiple Working: Blue Star Coupling Code.

Non-standard livery:
31116 is red, yellow, red and grey with 'Infrastructure' branding.

Originally numbered 5520–5699, 5800–5862 (not in order).

Class 31/1. Standard Design. RA5.

31102		C	LCXX	BS (U)
31106	*	C	LCWX	BS (U)
31107		C	LCWX	BS (U)
31110		C	LWNW	CD
31113		C	LWNW	CD
31116		O	ENXX	TO (U)
31119		C	LCWX	SP (U)
31125	.	C	LCXX	BS (U)
31126		C	LCWX	SP (U)
31128		FO	LCXX	BS (U)
31130		FC	LCWX	CD (U) Calder Hall Power Station
31132		FO	LCWX	BS (U)
31134		C	LCWX	SP (U)
31135		C	ENXX	TO (U)
31142		C	LWNW	CD
31144		C	LCWX	SP (U)
31145		C	LCXX	SP (U)
31146	r	C	LWNW	CD Brush Veteran
31147	r	C	LCWX	BS (U)
31149		FR	ENXX	TO (U)
31154		C	LWNW	CD
31155		FA	LCXX	BS (U)
31158		C	LCXX	BS (U)
31160		F	LCXX	SP (U)
31163		C	LWNW	CD
31164		FO	LCWX	BS (U)
31165		G	ENXX	TO (U)

31166	r	C	LWNW	CD
31171		FO	LCXX	BS (U)
31174		C	LCXX	BS (U)
31178		C	LCWX	BS (U)
31181		C	ENXX	TO (U)
31185		C	LCWX	CD (U)
31186		C	ENXX	TO (U)
31187		C	ENXX	TO (U)
31188		C	LWNW	CD
31190		C	LCWX	SP (U)
31191		C	ENXX	TO (U)
31199		FC	LCWX	SP (U)
31200		FC	LCXX	SP (U)
31201		FC	LWNW	CD
31203		C	LWNW	CD
31205		FR	ENXX	TO (U)
31206		C	LCWX	BS (U)
31207		C	LWNW	CD
31219		C	ENXX	TO (U)
31224		C	LCWX	SP (U)
31229		C	LWNW	CD
31230	*	FO	ENXX	TO (U)
31232		C	LCWX	BS (U)
31233		C	LWNW	CD Severn Valley Railway
31235		C	LCWX	SP (U)
31237		C	LCWX	BS (U)
31238		C	LCWX	SP (U)
31242		C	LCWX	SP (U)
31247		FR	ENXX	TO (U)
31248		FO	LCXX	BS (U)
31250		C	ENXX	TO (U)
31252		FO	ENXX	TO (U)
31255		C	LWNW	CD
31263		C	LCXX	SP (U)
31268		C	ENXX	TO (U)
31270		FC	LCWX	SP (U)
31271		FA	ENXX	TO (U)
31273		C	LWNW	CD
31275		FC	LCWX	CD (U)
31276		FC	ENXX	TO (U)
31285		C	LCWX	SP (U)
31294		FA	ENXX	TO (U)
31301		FR	LCXX	SP (U)
31302		FP	LCWX	SP (U)
31304		FC	LCXX	SP (U)
31306		C	LWNW	CD
31308		C	LWNW	CD
31312		FC	LCXX	SP (U)
31317		FO	LCWX	BS (U)
31319		FC	LCWX	CD (U)
31327		FR	LCWX	SP (U)

Class 31/4. Equipped with Train Heating. RA6.
Class 31/5. Train Heating Equipment isolated. RA6.

31405	M	LCWX	CD (U)	
31407	ML	LWNW	CD	
31408		LCXX	SP (U)	
31410	RR	LCWX	CD (U)	
31411	D	LCXX	BS (U)	
31512	C	LWNW	CD	
31514	C	LCWX	CD (U)	
31415		LCXX	BS (U)	
31516	C	LCXX	BS (U)	
31417	D	LCXX	BS (U)	
31519	C	LCXX	SP (U)	
31420	M	LWNW	CD	
31421	RR	LCWX	CD (U)	
31422	M	LCWX	BS (U)	
31423	M	LCWX	BS (U)	
31524	C	LCWX	BS (U)	
31526	C	LCXX	BS (U)	
31427		LCWX	SP (U)	
31530	C	LCWX	BS (U)	
31531	C	ENXX	TO (U)	
31432		LCWX	SP (U)	
31533	C	LCXX	BS (U)	
31434		LWNW	CD	
31435	C	LCWX	BS (U)	
31537	C	LCWX	BS (U)	
31538		LCWX	SP (U)	
31439	RR	LWNW	CD	North Yorkshire Moors Railway
31541	C	ENXX	TO (U)	
31444	C	LCXX	SP (U)	
31545		LCWX	CD (U)	
31546	C	LCWX	BS (U)	
31548	C	LCXX	BS (U)	
31549	C	ENXX	TO (U)	
31450		LWNW	CD	
31551	C	ENXX	TO (U)	
31552	C	ENXX	TO (U)	
31554	C	LWNW	CD	
31455	RR	LCWX	SP (U)	
31556	C	LCWX	SP (U)	
31558	C	ENXX	TO (U)	
31459		ENXX	TO (U)	
31461	D	ENXX	CD (U)	
31462	D	LCWX	CD (U)	
31563	C	ENXX	TO (U)	
31465	RR	LWNW	CD	
31466	C	LWNW	CD	
31467		LWNW	CD	
31468	C	LCWX	CD (U)	The Enginemen's Fund

CLASS 33   BRCW TYPE 3   Bo–Bo

Built: 1960–62 by the Birmingham Railway Carriage & Wagon Company, Smethwick.
Engine: Sulzer 8LDA28 of 1160 kW (1550 hp) at 750 rpm.
Main Generator: Crompton Parkinson CG391B1.
Traction Motors: Crompton Parkinson C171C2.
Max. Tractive Effort: 200 kN (45000 lbf).
Cont. Tractive Effort: 116 kN (26000 lbf) at 17.5 m.p.h.
Power At Rail: 906 kW (1215 hp).   **Length over Buffers:** 15.47 m.
Brake Force: 35 t.   **Wheel Diameter:** 1092 mm.
Design Speed: 85 m.p.h.   **Weight:** 77.5 t (78.5 t Class 33/1).
Max. Speed: 60 m.p.h.   **RA:** 6.
Train Heating: Electric (y isolated).   **ETH Index:** 48.
Train Brakes: Air & vacuum.
Multiple Working: Blue Star Coupling Code.

33116 carries its original number D 6535.

Originally numbered in series 6500–97 but not in order.

Class 33/0. Standard Design.

33019	e	C	EWDB	SL	
33025	e	C	EWDB	SL	
33026	e	C	EWDB	SL	
33030	e	C	EWDB	SL	
33046	y	C	EWDB	SL	
33051	e		EWDB	SL	Shakespeare Cliff

Class 33/1. Fitted with Buckeye Couplings & SR Multiple Working Equipment for use with SR EMUs, TC stock & class 73.
Also fitted with flashing light adaptor for use on Weymouth Quay line.

33116	e	EWDB	SL	Hertfordshire Rail Tours

Class 33/2. Built to Former Loading Gauge of Tonbridge–Battle Line.

33202	ys	C	EWDB	SL

CLASS 37   ENGLISH ELECTRIC TYPE 3   Co–Co

Built: 1960–5 by English Electric Company at Vulcan Foundry, Newton le Willows or Robert Stephenson & Hawthorn, Darlington. 37003–115/340/1/3/350/1/9 with the exception of 37019*/047/065*/072*/073/074/075*/100* (* one end only) retain box-type route indicators, the remainder having central headcode panels/marker lamps.
Engine: English Electric 12CSVT of 1300 kW (1750 hp) at 850 rpm.
Main Generator: English Electric 822/10G.
Traction Motors: English Electric 538/A.
Max. Tractive Effort: 245 kN (55500 lbf).
Cont. Tractive Effort: 156 kN (35000 lbf) at 13.6 m.p.h.
Power At Rail: 932 kW (1250 hp).   **Length over Buffers:** 18.75 m.
Brake Force: 50 t.   **Wheel Diameter:** 1092 mm.

Design Speed: 90 m.p.h.   **Weight:** 103–108 t.
Max. Speed: 80 m.p.h.   **RA:** 5 or 7.
Train Heating: Electric (Class 37/4 only). **ETH Index:** 30.
Train Brakes: Air & Vacuum.
Multiple Working: Blue Star Coupling Code.

Ownership:
37607–12 have recently been sold to Direct Rail Services but no pool code change has yet been made.

Non-standard livery:
37116 is BR blue with Transrail markings.

a Vacuum brake isolated.

Originally numbered 6600–8, 6700–6999 (not in order). 37274 is the second loco to carry that number. It was renumbered to avoid confusion with Class 37/3 locos.

Class 37/0. Unrefurbished Locos. Technical details as above. RA5.

37003	+	C	FDYX	IM (U)	
37010		C	ENTN	TO	
37012		C	LBSB	BS	
37013	+	ML	ENTN	TO	
37019	+	FD	FDYX	IM (U)	
37023		ML	EWDB	SF	Stratford TMD Quality Approved
37025		BR	LWCW	CD	Inverness TMD Quality Assured
37026	+	FD	LCWX	SP (U)	
37035		C	ENXX	SL (U)	
37037		FM	EWDB	SF	
37038		C	ENTN	TO	
37040		E	EWRB	SF	
37042	+	E	ENTN	TO	
37043		CT	LGBM	ML	
37045	+	F	LCWX	CF (U)	
37046		C	ENTN	TO	
37047	+	ML	EWDB	SF	
37048		FM	ENXX	TO (U)	
37051		E	ENTN	TO	Merehead
37054		C	EWDB	SF	
37055	+	ML	ENTN	TO	RAIL Celebrity
37057	+	E	ENTN	TO	Viking
37058	+	C	FDYX	IM (U)	
37059	+	FD	FDYX	IM (U)	
37063	+	FD	FDYX	TE (U)	
37065	+	ML	ENTN	TO	
37068	+	FD	FDYX	IM (U)	
37069	+	C	LGBM	ML	
37071	+	C	ENTN	TO	
37072	+	D	ENTN	TO	
37073	+	FT	LWCW	CD	Fort William/An Gearasdan
37074	+	ML	EWDB	SF	
37075	+	F	FDYX	TE (U)	

37077		ML	EWDB	SF
37078	+	FS	LCXX	ML (U)
37079	+	FD	ENTN	TO
37083	+	C	FDYX	IM (U)
37087		C	LCWX	CD
37088		CT	LCWX	ML (U) Clydesdale
37092		C	ENXX	TO (U)
37095	+	C	LWCW	CD
37097		C	ENTN	TO
37098	+	C	ENTN	TO
37100	+	FT	LGBM	ML
37101	+	FD	FDYX	IM (U)
37104		C	FDYX	IM (U)
37106	+	C	EWDB	SF
37107	+	FD	LCWX	SP (U)
37108	+	F	LCWX	BS (U)
37109		E	EWDB	SF
37110	+	F	FDYX	IM (U)
37111		FT	LCWX	BS (U)
37114	+	E	ENTN	TO City of Worcester
37116	+	O	LWCW	CD Sister Dora
37131	+	F	FDRI	IM
37133		C	EWDB	SF
37137		FM	ENXX	TO (U)
37139	+	FC	FDYX	IM (U)
37140		C	EWDB	SF
37141		C	LWCW	CD
37142		C	LCWX	CD (U)
37144	r	FA	FDYX	IM (U)
37146		C	LWCW	CD
37152		I	LGBM	ML
37153		CT	LGBM	ML
37154	+	FT	LBSB	BS
37156	r	FT	LCWX	ML (U)
37158		C	LWCW	CD
37162	+	D	ENTN	TO
37165	+	C	LGBM	ML
37167	+	ML	EWDB	SF
37170	r	C	LGBM	ML
37174		E	EWRB	SF
37175		C	LGBM	ML
37178	+	F	LCWX	BS (U)
37184		C	LCWX	BS (U)
37185	+	C	ENTN	TO Lea & Perrins
37188		C	LCWX	BS (U)
37191		C	LWCW	CD
37194	+	FM	EWRB	SF British International Freight Association
37196		C	LBSB	BS
37197	+	CT	LNSK	CF
37198	+	ML	EWDB	SF
37201		CT	LCWX	BS (U)

37203		**ML**	EWDB	SF
37207		**C**	LCWX	BS (U)
37209		**BR**	FDYX	IM (U)
37211		**C**	LWCW	CD
37212	+	**FT**	LWCW	CD
37213	+	**FC**	LCWX	CF (U)
37214	+	**FT**	LCWX	CD (U)
37216	r+	**ML**	EWDB	SF	Great Eastern
37217	+		FDYX	IM (U)
37218	+	**F**	FDYX	IM (U)
37219	r	**ML**	EWDB	SF
37220	+	**E**	EWRB	SF
37221		**FT**	LGBM	ML
37222	+	**FM**	ENTN	TO
37223	+	**FC**	FDYX	IM (U)
37225	+	**F**	FDRI	IM
37227	+	**FM**	ENXX	TO (U)
37229	+	**FC**	LNSK	CF
37230	+	**CT**	LNSK	CF
37232	r	**CT**	LCWX	ML (U)	The Institution of Railway Signal Engineers
37235	+	**F**	FDYX	IM (U)
37238	+	**F**	ENTN	TO
37240	+	**C**	LCWX	CD (U)
37241		**F**	ENXX	SF (U)
37242	+	**ML**	EWDB	SF
37244	+	**F**	ENTN	TO
37245		**C**	EWRB	SF
37248	+	**ML**	ENTN	TO	Midland Railway Centre
37250	+	**FT**	LGBM	ML
37251	+	**I**	LCWX	ML (U)	The Northern Lights
37254	+	**C**	LNSK	CF
37255	+	**C**	LBSB	BS
37258	+	**C**	LBSB	BS
37261	+	**FD**	LGBM	ML	Caithness
37262	+	**D**	EWDB	SF
37263		**C**	LNSK	CF
37264		**C**	ENTN	TO
37274	+	**ML**	EWDB	SF
37275	+		LNSK	CF	Oor Wullie
37278	+	**FC**	ENXX	TO (U)
37293	+	**ML**	EWRB	SF
37294	+	**C**	LGBM	ML
37298	+	**F**	FDYX	IM (U)

Class 37/3. Unrefurbished locos fitted with regeared (CP7) bogies.
Details as Class 37/0 except:

Max. Tractive Effort: 250 kN (56180 lbf).
Cont. Tractive Effort: 184 kN (41250 lbf) at 11.4 m.p.h.

37330	+	**BR**	FDYX	IM (U)

37331		F	FDYX	IM (U)	
37332	+	FC	FDRI	IM	The Coal Merchants'
					Association of Scotland
37334	+	F	LCWX	BS (U)	
37335	+	F	FDYX	IM (U)	
37340	+	FD	FDYX	IM (U)	
37341	+	F	FDYX	TE (U)	
37343		C	FDYX	IM (U)	
37344	+	FD	FDYX	IM (U)	
37350	+	FP	FDRI	IM	
37351	+	CT	LGBM	ML	
37358		F	FDYX	IM (U)	
37359		FP	FDYX	TE (U)	
37370		E	EWRB	SF	
37371	+	ML	EWDB	SF	
37372		ML	EWRB	SF	
37375	+	C	EWDB	SF	
37376	+	FC	ENTN	TO	
37377	+	C	EWDB	SF	
37379		ML	EWDB	SF	Ipswich WRD Quality Assured
37380		FM	EWRB	SF	
37381	+	FD	FDYX	IM (U)	
37382		FP	FDYX	IM (U)	

Class 37/4. Refurbished locos fitted with train heating. Main generator replaced by alternator. Regeared (CP7) bogies. Details as class 37/0 except:

Main Alternator: Brush BA1005A.
Max. Tractive Effort: 256 kN (57440 lbf).
Cont. Tractive Effort: 184 kN (41250 lbf) at 11.4 m.p.h.
Power At Rail: 935 kW (1254 hp).
All have twin fuel tanks.

37401	r	FT	LGHM	ML	Mary Queen of Scots
37402	r	F	LWCW	CD	Bont Y Bermo
37403	r	G	LGHM	ML	Ben Cruachan
37404	r	FT	LGHM	ML	Loch Long
37405	r	E	EWDB	SF	Strathclyde Region
37406	r	FT	LGHM	ML	The Saltaire Society
37407	r	FT	LWCW	CD	Blackpool Tower
37408		BR	LWCW	CD	Loch Rannoch
37409	r	FT	LGHM	ML	Loch Awe
37410	r	FT	LGHM	ML	Aluminium 100
37411		E	LNCK	CF	Ty Hafan
37412		FT	LNCK	CF	Driver John Elliot
37413	r	FT	LGHM	ML	Loch Eil Outward Bound
37414	r	RR	LWMC	CD	Cathays C&W Works 1846–1993
37415	r	E	LWMC	CD	
37416	r	E	LNCK	CF	
37417	r	F	LWCW	CD	Highland Region
37418	r	E	LWMC	CD	East Lancashire Railway
37419		E	LWMC	CD	

37420	r	**RR**	LWMC	CD	The Scottish Hosteller
37421	r	**E**	LWMC	CD	The Kingsman
37422	r	**RR**	LWMC	CD	Robert F. Fairlie Locomotive
					Engineer 1831–1885
37423	r	**FT**	EWDB	SF	Sir Murray Morrison 1873–1948
					Pioneer of British Aluminium Industry
37424	r	**FT**	LGHM	ML	
37425	r	**RR**	LWMC	CD	Sir Robert McAlpine/
					Concrete Bob (opposite sides)
37426	r	**E**	LWMC	CD	
37427	r	**E**	LNCK	CF	
37428	r	**F**	LGHM	ML	David Lloyd George
37429	r	**RR**	LWMC	CD	Eisteddfod Genedlaethol
37430	r	**FT**	LGHM	ML	Cwmbrân
37431	r	**M**	ENTN	TO	

Class 37/5. Refurbished locos. Main generator replaced by alternator.
Regeared (CP7) bogies. Details as class 37/4 except:

Max. Tractive Effort: 248 kN (55590 lbf).
All have twin fuel tanks.

37503		**E**	FDCI	IM	
37505		**FT**	LWCW	CD	British Steel Workington
37509		**F**	LWCW	CD	
37510		**I**	LGBM	ML	
37513		**LH**	FDCI	IM	
37515	s	**FS**	FDCI	IM	
37516	s	**LH**	FDCI	IM	
37517	ars	**E**	FDCI	IM	
37518		**E**	LWCW	CD	
37519		**FS**	FDCI	IM	
37520		**E**	LWCW	CD	
37521		**E**	LNLK	CF	English China Clays

Class 37/6. Refurbished locos for use on Channel Tunnel Night services.
All have train air brakes only, UIC brake and coaching stock jumpers, RCH
jumpers, ETH through wires.

37601	(37501)	**EP**	GPSV	OC	
37602	(37502)	**EP**	GPSV	OC	
37603	(37504)	**EP**	GPSV	OC	
37604	(37506)	**EP**	GPSV	OC	
37605	(37507)	**EP**	GPSV	OC	
37606	(37508)	**EP**	GPSV	OC	
37607	(37511)	**EP**		SD	
37608	(37512)	**EP**		SD	
37609	(37514)	**EP**		SD	
37610	(37687)	**EP**		SD	
37611	(37690)	**EP**		SD	
37612	(37691)	**EP**		SD	

Class 37/5 continued.

37667	s	E	LWCW	CD	Meldon Quarry Centenary
37668	s	E	LNLK	CF	
37669		E	LNLK	CF	
37670		FT	LNLK	CF	St. Blazey T&RS Depot
37671		FT	LNLK	CF	Tre Pol and Pen
37672	s	FD	LNLK	CF	
37673		FT	LNLK	CF	
37674		FT	LNLK	CF	Saint Blaise Church 1445–1995
37675	s	FT	LGBM	ML	
37676		F	EWDB	SF	
37677		F	FDCI	IM	
37678		F	LWCW	CD	
37679		F	EWDB	SF	
37680		FA	FDCI	IM	
37682	r	E	FDCI	IM	Hartlepool Pipe Mill
37683		FT	LGBM	ML	
37684		E	FDCI	IM	Peak National Park
37685		I	LGBM	ML	
37686		FA	FDCI	IM	
37688		E	FDCI	IM	
37689	s	F	FDCI	IM	
37692	s	FC	LGBM	ML	The Lass O' Ballochmyle
37693	s	FT	LGBM	ML	
37694	s	E	FDCI	IM	
37695	s	E	LWCW	CD	
37696	s	FT	LNLK	CF	
37697	s	E	FDCI	JM	
37698	s	LH	FDCI	IM	

Class 37/7. Refurbished locos. Main generator replaced by alternator. Regeared (CP7) bogies. Ballast weights added. Details as class 37/4 except:

Main Alternator: GEC G564AZ (37796–803) Brush BA1005A (others).
Max. Tractive Effort: 276 kN (62000 lbf).
Weight: 120 t.   **RA:** 7.
All have twin fuel tanks.

37701	s	FT	LNCK	CF	
37702	s	FT	LGBM	ML	Taff Merthyr
37703	s	E	EWDB	SF	
37704	s	E	LNCK	CF	
37705		FM	EWDB	SF	
37706		E	FDCI	IM	
37707		E	FDCI	IM	
37708		FP	FDCI	IM	
37709		FM	EWDB	SF	
37710		LH	FDCI	IM	
37711		FS	EWDB	SF	
37712		E	LGBM	ML	Teesside Steelmaster
37713		LH	FDCI	IM	

37714		E	LGBM	ML	
37715		FM	ENTN	TO	British Petroleum
37716		E	FDCI	IM	British Steel Corby
37717		E	FDCI	IM	Maltby Lilly Hall Junior School Rotherham Railsafe Trophy Winners 1996
37718		E	FDCI	IM	
37719		FP	FDCI	IM	
37796	s	FC	LGBM	ML	
37797	s	FC	LGBM	ML	
37798	s	ML	ENTN	TO	
37799	s	FT	LGBM	ML	Sir Dyfed/County of Dyfed
37800	s	E	EWDB	SF	
37801	s	E	LGBM	ML	
37802	s	FT	LGBM	ML	
37803	s	ML	EWDB	SF	
37883		E	FDCI	IM	
37884		LH	FDCI	IM	Gartcosh
37885		E	FDCI	IM	
37886		E	FDCI	IM	
37887	s	FT	LNCK	CF	
37888		F	LNCK	CF	
37889		FT	LNCK	CF	
37890	a	FM	EWDB	SF	The Railway Observer
37891		FM	EWDB	SF	
37892		FM	EWDB	SF	Ripple Lane
37893		E	LGBM	ML	
37894	s	FC	LNCK	CF	
37895	s	E	LNCK	CF	
37896	s	FT	LNCK	CF	
37897	s	FT	LNCK	CF	
37898	s	FT	LNCK	CF	Cwmbargoed DP
37899	s	E	LNCK	CF	County of West Glamorgan/ Sir Gorllewin Morgannwg

Class 37/9. Refurbished Locos. Fitted with manufacturers prototype power units and ballast weights. Main generator replaced by alternator. Details as Class 37/0 except:

Engine: Mirrlees MB275T of 1340 kW (1800 hp) at 1000 rpm (37901–4), Ruston RK270T of 1340 kW (1800 hp) at 900 rpm (37905–6).
Main Alternator: Brush BA1005A (GEC G564, 37905/6).
Max. Tractive Effort: 279 kN (62680 lbf).
Cont. Tractive Effort: 184 kN (41250 lbf) at 11.4 m.p.h.
Weight: 120 t.   **RA:** 7.
All have twin fuel tanks.

37901		FT	LNCK	CF	Mirrlees Pioneer
37902		FS	LNCK	CF	
37903		FS	LNCK	CF	
37904		FS	LCWX	CF (U)	
37905	s	FS	LCWX	CF (U)	
37906	s	FT	LCWX	CF (U)	

CLASS 43   HST POWER CAR   Bo–Bo

Built: 1976–82 by BREL Crewe Works. Formerly numbered as coaching stock but now classified as locomotives. Fitted with luggage compartment.
Engine: Paxman Valenta 12RP200L (Paxman VP185*) of 1680 kW (2250 hp) at 1500 rpm.
Main Alternator: Brush BA1001B.
Traction Motors: Brush TMH68–46 or GEC G417AZ (43124–151/180). Frame mounted.
Max. Tractive Effort: 80 kN (17980 lbf).
Cont. Tractive Effort: 46 kN (10340 lbf) at 64.5 m.p.h.
Power At Rail: 1320 kW (1770 hp).   **ETH:** Non standard 3-phase system.
Brake Force: 35 t.   **Length over Buffers:** 17.79 m.
Weight: 70 t.   **Wheel Diameter:** 1020 mm.
Max. Speed: 125 m.p.h.   **RA:** 5.
Train Brakes: Air.
Multiple Working: With one other similar vehicle.
Communication Equipment: All equipped with driver–guard telephone.

Ownership:
Midland Mainline and Virgin Cross Country power cars are owned by Porterbrook Leasing Company. Great North Eastern Railway, Great Western Trains and Virgin West Coast power cars are owned by Angel Train contracts.

§ Modified to be able to remotely control a class 91 locomotive and to be remotely controlled by a class 91 locomotive. Fitted with buffers. Tdm and Class 91 control equipment now isolated.
43180 is a spare power which is used to cover for failures and shortages.

43002		IWRP	PM	
43003	GW	IWRP	PM	
43004	GW	IWRP	PM	Borough of Swindon
43005	GW	IWRP	PM	
43006	I	IWRP	LA	
43007	I	IWRP	LA	
43008	GW	IWRP	LA	
43009	I	IWRP	PM	
43010	GW	IWRP	PM	
43011	GW	IWRP	PM	Reader 125
43012	GW	IWRP	PM	
43013 §	I	ICCS	EC	CROSSCOUNTRY VOYAGER
43014 §	I	ICCS	EC	
43015	GW	IWRP	PM	
43016	I	IWRP	PM	
43017	GW	IWRP	LA	
43018	GW	IWRP	LA	
43019	I	IWRP	LA	City of Swansea/Dinas Abertawe
43020	GW	IWRP	LA	John Grooms
43021	I	IWRP	LA	
43022	I	IWRP	LA	
43023	I	IWRP	LA	County of Cornwall
43024	I	IWRP	LA	

43025		I	IWRP	LA	Exeter
43026		GW	IWRP	LA	City of Westminster
43027		I	IWRP	LA	Glorious Devon
43028		I	IWCP	LO	
43029		I	IWCP	LO	
43030		GW	IWRP	PM	
43031		I	IWRP	PM	
43032		GW	IWRP	PM	The Royal Regiment of Wales
43033		I	IWRP	PM	
43034		I	IWRP	PM	The Black Horse
43035		I	IWRP	PM	
43036		I	IWRP	PM	
43037		I	IWRP	PM	
43038		GN	IECP	NL	
43039		GN	IECP	NL	
43040		I	IWRP	PM	
43041		I	IWCP	LO	City of Discovery
43042		I	IWCP	LO	
43043		MM	IMLP	NL	LEICESTERSHIRE COUNTY CRICKET CLUB
43044		I	IMLP	NL	Borough of Kettering
43045		I	IMLP	NL	The Grammar School Doncaster AD 1350
43046		I	IMLP	NL	Royal Philharmonic
43047	*	I	IMLP	NL	Rotherham Enterprise
43048		I	IMLP	NL	
43049		MM	IMLP	NL	Neville Hill
43050		I	IMLP	NL	
43051		I	IMLP	NL	The Duke and Duchess of York
43052		I	IMLP	NL	City of Peterborough
43053		I	IMLP	NL	Leeds United
43054		I	IMLP	NL	
43055		I	IMLP	NL	Sheffield Star
43056		I	IMLP	NL	University of Bradford
43057		I	IMLP	NL	Bounds Green
43058		MM	IMLP	NL	
43059	*	MM	IMLP	NL	MIDLAND PRIDE
43060		I	IMLP	NL	County of Leicestershire
43061		I	IMLP	NL	City of Lincoln
43062		I	ICCS	EC	
43063		V	ICCS	EC	Maiden Voyager
43064		I	IMLP	NL	City of York
43065	§	I	ICCS	EC	City of Edinburgh
43066		MM	IMLP	NL	Nottingham Playhouse
43067	§	I	ICCS	EC	
43068	§	V	ICCS	EC	The Red Nose
43069		I	ICCS	EC	
43070		I	ICCS	EC	
43071		I	ICCS	EC	Forward Birmingham
43072		I	IMLP	NL	Derby Etches Park
43073		I	IMLP	NL	
43074	*	MM	IMLP	NL	BBC EAST MIDLANDS TODAY
43075	*	I	IMLP	NL	

43076	**MM**	IMLP	NL	
43077	**MM**	IMLP	NL	
43078	**I**	ICCS	EC	Golowan Festival Penzance
43079	**I**	ICCS	EC	
43080 §	**I**	ICCS	EC	
43081	**I**	IMLP	NL	
43082	**I**	IMLP	NL	
43083	**I**	IMLP	NL	
43084 §	**I**	ICCS	EC	County of Derbyshire
43085	**I**	IMLP	NL	City of Bradford
43086	**I**	ICCS	EC	
43087	**I**	ICCP	LA	
43088	**I**	ICCP	LA	XIII Commonwealth Games Scotland 1986
43089	**I**	ICCP	LA	
43090	**I**	ICCP	LA	
43091	**I**	ICCP	LA	Edinburgh Military Tattoo
43092	**V**	ICCS	EC	Institution of Mechanical Engineers 150th Anniversary 1847-1997
43093	**V**	ICCS	EC	Lady in Red
43094	**I**	ICCS	EC	
43095	**GN**	IECP	NL	
43096	**GN**	IECP	NL	The Great Racer
43097	**I**	ICCS	EC	
43098	**I**	ICCS	EC	
43099	**I**	ICCS	EC	
43100	**I**	ICCS	EC	Craigentinny
43101	**I**	ICCP	LA	Edinburgh International Festival
43102	**I**	ICCP	LA	
43103	**I**	ICCP	LA	John Wesley
43104	**I**	SCXL	NL	County of Cleveland
43105	**GN**	IECP	NL	
43106	**GN**	IECP	NL	
43107	**GN**	IECP	NL	
43108	**GN**	IECP	NL	
43109	**GN**	IECP	NL	
43110	**GN**	IECP	EC	
43111	**GN**	IECP	EC	
43112	**GN**	IECP	EC	
43113	**GN**	IECP	EC	
43114	**GN**	IECP	EC	
43115	**GN**	IECP	EC	
43116	**GN**	IECP	EC	
43117	**GN**	IECP	EC	
43118	**GN**	IECP	EC	
43119	**GN**	IECP	EC	
43120	**GN**	IECP	EC	
43121	**I**	ICCP	LA	West Yorkshire Metropolitan County
43122	**I**	ICCP	LA	South Yorkshire Metropolitan County
43123 §	**I**	ICCS	EC	
43124	**GW**	IWRP	PM	
43125	**I**	IWRP	PM	Merchant Venturer

43126	I	IWRP	PM	City of Bristol
43127	I	IWRP	PM	
43128	I	IWRP	PM	
43129	GW	IWRP	PM	
43130	I	IWRP	PM	Sulis Minerva
43131	GW	IWRP	PM	Sir Felix Pole
43132	GW	IWRP	PM	
43133	I	IWRP	PM	
43134	I	IWRP	PM	County of Somerset
43135	GW	IWRP	PM	
43136	GW	IWRP	PM	
43137	GW	IWRP	PM	Newton Abbot 150
43138	GW	IWRP	PM	
43139	GW	IWRP	PM	
43140	GW	IWRP	PM	
43141	GW	IWRP	PM	
43142	GW	IWRP	PM	
43143	I	IWRP	PM	
43144	I	IWRP	PM	
43145	I	IWRP	PM	
43146	I	IWRP	PM	
43147	I	IWRP	PM	The Red Cross
43148	I	IWRP	PM	
43149	I	IWRP	PM	BBC Wales Today
43150	I	IWRP	PM	Bristol Evening Post
43151	I	IWRP	PM	
43152	I	IWRP	PM	
43153	V	ICCP	LA	THE ENGLISH RIVIERA TORQUAY PAIGNTON BRIXHAM INTERCITY
43154	I	ICCP	LA	
43155	V	ICCP	LA	The Red Arrows
43156	I	ICCP	LA	
43157	I	ICCP	LA	Yorkshire Evening Post
43158	I	ICCP	LA	Dartmoor The Pony Express
43159	I	ICCP	LA	
43160	I	ICCP	LA	Storm Force
43161	I	ICCP	LA	Reading Evening Post
43162	I	ICCP	LA	Borough of Stevenage
43163	I	IWRP	LA	
43164	I	IWCP	LO	
43165	I	IWCP	LO	
43166	I	IWCP	LO	
43167	* GN	IECP	NL	
43168	* GW	IWRP	LA	
43169	* I	IWRP	LA	The National Trust
43170	* GW	IWRP	LA	Edward Paxman
43171	I	IWRP	LA	
43172	I	IWRP	LA	
43173	I	IWRP	LA	Swansea University
43174	GW	IWRP	LA	Bristol - Bordeaux
43175	I	IWRP	LA	

43176	I	IWRP	LA	
43177	* GW	IWRP	LA	University of Exeter
43178	I	IWRP	LA	
43179	GW	IWRP	LA	Pride of Laira
43180	I	IMLP	NL	
43181	I	IWRP	LA	Devonport Royal Dockyard 1693-1993
43182	GW	IWRP	LA	
43183	GW	IWRP	LA	
43184	I	IWRP	LA	
43185	GW	IWRP	LA	Great Western
43186	GW	IWRP	LA	Sir Francis Drake
43187	GW	IWRP	LA	
43188	GW	IWRP	LA	City of Plymouth
43189	GW	IWRP	LA	RAILWAY HERITAGE TRUST
43190	GW	IWRP	LA	
43191	GW	IWRP	LA	Seahawk
43192	GW	IWRP	LA	City of Truro
43193	I	ICCP	LA	Plymouth SPIRIT OF DISCOVERY
43194	I	ICCP	LA	
43195	I	ICCP	LA	British Red Cross 125th Birthday 1995
43196	I	ICCP	LA	The Newspaper Society Founded 1836
43197	I	ICCP	LA	Railway Magazine 1897 Centenary 1997
43198	I	ICCP	LA	

CLASS 46   BR TYPE 4   1Co–Co1

Built: 1962 by BR Derby Locomotive Works.
Engine: Sulzer 12LDA28B of 1860 kW (2500 hp) at 750 rpm.
Main Generator: Brush TG160-60.
Traction Motors: Brush TM73-68 Mk3 (axle hung).
Max. Tractive Effort: 245 kN (55000 lbf).
Cont. Tractive Effort: 141 kN (31600 lbf) at 22.3 m.p.h.
Power At Rail: 1460 kW (1960 hp).   **Length over Buffers:** 20.70 m.
Brake Force: 63 t.   **Wheel Diameter:** 914/1143 mm.
Design Speed: 90 m.p.h.   **Weight:** 141 t.
Max. Speed: 75 m.p.h.   **RA:** 7.
Train Brakes: Air & vacuum.
Multiple Working: Not equipped.

Ownership:
Owned by London & North Western Railway Company Ltd.

Carries original number D 172.

46035	G	MBDL	CQ	Ixion

CLASS 47   BRUSH TYPE 4   Co–Co

Built: 1963–67 by Brush Traction, Loughborough or BR Crewe Works.
Engine: Sulzer 12LDA28C of 1920 kW (2580 hp) at 750 rpm.
Main Generator: Brush TG160-60 Mk2, TG160-60 Mk4 or TM172-50 Mk1.
Traction Motors: Brush TM64-68 Mk1 or Mk1A (axle hung).
Max. Tractive Effort: 267 kN (60000 lbf).
Cont. Tractive Effort: 133 kN (30000 lbf) at 26 m.p.h.
Power At Rail: 1550 kW (2080 hp).   **Length over Buffers:** 19.38 m.
Brake Force: 61 t.   **Wheel Diameter:** 1143 mm.
Design Speed: 95 m.p.h.   **Weight:** 120.5–125 t.
Max. Speed: various.   **RA:** 6 or 7.
Train Brakes: Air & vacuum.
Multiple Working: Green Circle (m) or Blue Star (*) Coupling Code. Otherwise not equipped.
ETH Index (47/4, 47/6 and 47/7): 66 (75 Class 47/6).

Ownership:
Freightliner 1995 locos nos. 47052/60/142/7/57/87/97/206/12/25/31/70/9/83/9/96/301/5/17/22/37/9/45/7/9/54/8/71/6/7 plus Great Western Trains and Virgin locos are owned by Porterbrook Leasing Company.
47488/703/9/10/2 are owned by Fragonset Railways.
47701 is owned by Alan and Tracey Lear and managed by Fragonset Railways.
47705 is owned by London & North Western Railway Company Ltd.

Non-standard liveries:
47114 is two-tone green with Freightliner lettering and markings.
47145 is dark blue with Railfreight Distribution markings.
47798/9 are Royal train purple.
47803 is grey, red and yellow.

a Vacuum brake isolated.

Formerly numbered 1100–11, 1500–1999 not in order.

Class 47/0. Built with train heating boiler. RA6. Max. Speed 75 m.p.h.

47004	**G**	ENRN	TO	Old Oak Common Traction & Rolling Stock Depot
47016	**FO**	LWCW	CD	ATLAS
47033	am+ **FE**	DAET	TI	The Royal Logistics Corps
47049	am+ **FE**	DAET	TI	GEFCO
47051	am+ **FE**	DAET	TI	
47052	**FF**	DFLR	CD	
47053	am+ **FE**	DAET	TI	Dollands Moor International
47060	a **F**	DFLT	CD	
47079	**FF**	DFLT	CD	
47085	am+ **FE**	DAET	TI	REPTA 1893–1993
47095	am+ **FE**	DAET	TI	
47114	am+ **0**	DFLM	CD	Freightlinerbulk
47125	am+ **FE**	DAET	TI	
47142	**FR**	DHLT	CD	

47144	am+	FD	DAXT	TI	
47145	am+	0	DAET	TI	
47146	am	FE	DAET	TI	Loughborough Grammar School
47147		F	DHLT	CD	
47150	am+	FE	DAET	TI	
47152	am+	FF	DFLM	CD	
47156	am+	FD	DHLT	CD (U)	
47157		FF	DFLR	CD	Johnson Stevens Agencies
47186	am+	FE	DAET	TI	Catcliffe Demon
47187		F	DHLT	CD	
47188	am+	FE	DAXT	TI	
47193		FP	LCWX	BS (U)	
47194	am+	FD	DAET	TI	
47197		FF	DFLT	CD	
47200	am+	FE	DAET	TI	Herbert Austin
47201	am+	FE	DAET	TI	
47204	am+	F	DFLM	CD	
47205	am+	FF	DFLM	CD	
47206		FF	DFLR	CD	The Morris Dancer
47207		F	DFLT	CD	
47209	am+	FF	DFLR	CD	
47210	am+	FD	DAET	TI	
47211	am+	FD	DAET	TI	
47212	+	FF	DFLR	CD	
47213	am+	FD	DAET	TI	Marchwood Military Port
47217	am+	FE	DAET	TI	
47218	am+	FE	DAET	TI	United Transport Europe
47219	am+	FE	DAET	TI	Arnold Kunzler
47221	+	FP	FDYX	IM (U)	
47222	am+	FD	DAYX	TI (U)	
47223	+	F	ENXX	SF (U)	
47224	+	FP	FDYX	IM (U)	
47225		FF	DFLR	CD	
47226	am+	FD	DAET	TI	
47228	am+	FE	DAET	TI	axial
47229	am+	FE	DAET	TI	
47231		FF	DFLT	CD	
47234	am+	FF	DFLM	CD	
47236	am+	FE	DAET	TI	ROVER GROUP QUALITY ASSURED
47237	am+	FE	DAET	TI	
47238		FD	LCXX	BS (U)	
47241	am+	FE	DAET	TI	Halewood Silver Jubilee 1988
47245	am+	FE	DAET	TI	The Institute of Export
47256		FD	FDYX	IM (U)	
47258	am+	FE	DAET	TI	
47270		FF	DHLT	CD	Cory Brothers 1842–1992
47276	am+	FD	DAET	TI	
47277		FD	FDYX	IM (U)	
47278		FP	ENXX	SF (U)	
47279	am+	FF	DFLM	CD	
47280	am+	FD	DAET	TI	Pedigree

47281 am+	FD	DAET	TI	
47283	F	DFLT	CD	
47284 am+	FD	DAET	TI	
47285 am+	FE	DAET	TI	
47286 am+	FE	DAET	TI	Port of Liverpool
47287 am+	FE	DAET	TI	
47289 a	FF	DFLT	CD	
47290 am+	FF	DFLR	CD	
47291 am+	FD	DAYX	TI (U)	
47292 am+	FD	DFLM	CD	
47293 am+	FE	DAET	TI	
47294 +	FD	FDYX	IM (U)	
47295 +	FP	LCWX	BS (U)	
47296	FF	DFLR	CD	
47297 am+	FE	DAET	TI	Cobra RAILFREIGHT
47298 am+	FD	DAET	TI	Pegasus
47299 am+	FE	DAXT	TI	

Class 47/3. Built without Train Heat. (except 47300). RA6. Max. Speed 75 m.p.h. All equipped with slow speed control.

47300	C	LCWX	BS (U)	
47301	FF	DFLR	CD	Freightliner Birmingham
47302 a	FR	DFLT	CD	
47303 am+	FF	DFLM	CD	Freightliner Cleveland
47304 am+	FD	DAET	TI	
47305	FF	DFLR	CD	
47306 am+	FE	DAET	TI	The Sapper
47307 am+	FE	DAET	TI	
47308	C	LCWX	BS (U)	
47309 am+	FD	DAET	TI	The Halewood Transmission
47310 am+	FE	DAET	TI	Henry Ford
47312 am+	FE	DAET	TI	
47313 am+	FD	DAET	TI	
47314 am+	FD	DAET	TI	Transmark
47315	C	FDKI	IM	
47316 am+	FE	DAXT	TI	
47317	F	DFLT	CD	
47319 +	FP	FDYX	IM (U)	Norsk Hydro
47322	FR	DHLT	CD	
47323 am+	FF	DFLR	CD	
47326 am+	FE	DAET	TI	Saltley Depot Quality Approved
47328 am+	FD	DAXT	TI	
47329	C	LCWX	BS (U)	
47330 am+	FD	DFLM	CD	
47331	C	FDKI	IM	
47332	C	LCWX	BS (U)	
47333	C	LCWX	BS (U)	
47334	C	LCWX	BS (U)	
47335 am+	FD	DAET	TI	
47337 am+	FF	DFLR	CD	
47338 am+	FE	DAET	TI	

47339		FF	DFLR	CD	
47340		C	DHLT	CD	
47341		C	LCWX	BS (U)	
47344	am+	FE	DAET	TI	
47345		FF	DFLR	CD	
47346		C	FDYX	IM (U)	
47347	a	F	DHLT	CD (U)	
47348	am	FE	DAET	TI	St. Christopher's Railway Home
47349		FF	DFLT	CD	
47350		FO	DHLT	CD	
47351	am+	FE	DAET	TI	
47352		C	FDYX	IM (U)	
47353		C	LCWX	BS (U)	
47354	a	FF	DFLR	CD	
47355	am+	FD	DAET	TI	
47356		FO	DHLT	CD	
47357		C	LCXX	BS (U)	
47358		FF	DFLT	CD	
47359		FD	FDYX	IM (U)	
47360	am+	FE	DAET	TI	
47361	am+	FF	DFLM	CD	
47362	am+	FD	DAET	TI	
47363	am+	F	DAET	TI	
47365	am+	FE	DAET	TI	ICI Diamond Jubilee
47366		C	ENXX	TO (U)	
47367		FR	DHLT	CD	
47368		F	ENXX	SF (U)	
47369		FD	FDYX	IM (U)	
47370		FF	DFLR	CD	Andrew A Hodgkinson
47371		FF	DFLR	CD	
47372		C	LCWX	BS (U)	
47375	am+	FE	DAET	TI	Tinsley Traction Depot
					Quality Approved
47376		FF	DFLR	CD	Freightliner 1995
47377	a	FF	DFLR	CD	
47378	am+	FD	DAXT	TI	
47379	am+	F	DAET	TI	

Class 47/4. Equipped with train heating. RA6. Max. Speed 95 m.p.h.

47462		R	ENXX	SF (U)	
47467		BR	PXLC	CD	
47471		IO	PXXA	CD (U)	
47473		BR	DHLT	CD	
47474		R	PXXA	CD (U)	Sir Rowland Hill
47475		RX	LWCW	CD	Restive
47476		R	FDKI	IM	Night Mail
47478			LCWX	BS (U)	
47481		BR	PXXA	CD (U)	
47484		G	ENXX	SF (U)	ISAMBARD KINGDOM BRUNEL
47488		W		TS (U)	DAVIES THE OCEAN
47489		R	PXXA	CD	

47492	RX	PXLC	CD	
47501	R	PXLC	CD	Craftsman
47513	BR	LCWX	CD (U)	Severn
47519	+ G	ENRN	TO	
47520	I	LWCW	CD	
47522	R	FDYX	IM (U)	Doncaster Enterprise
47523	M	LWCW	CD	
47524	RX	LCWX	CD (U)	
47525	FE	DAET	TI	
47526	BR	ENXX	SF (U)	
47528	M	LWCW	CD	The Queen's Own Mercian Yeomanry
47530	RX	LCWX	CD (S)	
47532	RX	LCWX	CD (S)	
47535	RX	LWCW	CD	
47536	RX	LCWX	CD (S)	
47539	RX	PXXA	CD	
47540	C	DAET	TI	The Institution of Civil Engineers
47543	R	FDKI	IM	
47547	N	PXXA	CD (U)	
47550	M	FDYX	IM (U)	University of Dundee
47555	FE	DAYX	TI	The Commonwealth Spirit
47565	RX	PXLC	CD	Responsive
47566	RX	LCWX	CD (U)	
47572	R	PXLC	CD	Ely Cathedral
47574	R	FDYX	IM (U)	Benjamin Gimbert G.C.
47575	R	PXLC	CD	City of Hereford
47576	RX	LCWX	CD (U)	
47584	RX	PXLC	CD	THE LOCOMOTIVE & CARRIAGE INSTITUTION
47596	RX	PXLC	CD	
47624	RX	PXLC	CD	Saint Andrew
47627	RX	PXLC	CD	
47628 j	RX	LCWX	CD (U)	
47634	R	PXLC	CD	Holbeck
47635 j	R	PXLC	CD	
47640 j	R	PXLC	CD	University of Strathclyde

Class 47/6. Fitted with high phosphorus brake blocks. RA6. Max. Speed 75 m.p.h.

| 47676 | I | FDYX | IM (U) | |
| 47677 | I | FDYX | IM (U) | |

Class 47/7. Fitted with an older form of TDM. RA6. Max. Speed 95 m.p.h. All have twin fuel tanks.

47701	RX		TS (U)	Waverley
47702	F	ENRN	TO	County of Suffolk
47703	W		TS (U)	LEWIS CARROLL
47704	RX	LCWX	CD (U)	
47705	W		CQ (U)	GUY FAWKES
47709	RX		TS (U)	
47710	W		TS (U)	

47711		N	LWCW	CD	County of Hertfordshire
47712		W		TS (U)	DICK WHITTINGTON
47715		N	LCWX	CD (S)	
47716		RX	LCWX	CD (S)	
47717		R	PXXA	CD (U)	

Class 47/7. Railnet dedicated locos. RA6. Max. Speed 95 m.p.h. All have twin fuel tanks and are fitted with RCH jumper cables for operating with propelling control vehicles (PCVs).

47721		RX	PXLB	CD	Saint Bede
47722	a	RX	PXLB	CD (U)	The Queen Mother
47725		RX	PXLB	CD	The Railway Mission
47726		RX	PXLB	CD	Progress
47727	a	RX	PXLB	CD	Duke of Edinburgh's Award
47732		RX	PXLB	CD	Restormel
47733	a	RX	PXLB	CD	Eastern Star
47734		RX	PXLB	CD	Crewe Diesel Depot Quality Approved
47736	a	RX	PXLB	CD	Cambridge Traction & Rolling Stock Depot
47737		RX	PXLB	CD	Resurgent
47738	a	RX	PXLB	CD	Bristol Barton Hill
47739	a	RX	PXLB	CD	Resourceful
47741		RX	PXLB	CD	Resilient
47742		RX	PXLB	CD	The Enterprising Scot
47744	a	RX	PXLB	CD	Saint Edwin
47745		RX	PXLB	CD	Royal London Society for the Blind
47746	a	RX	PXLB	CD	The Bobby
47747	a	RX	PXLB	CD	Res Publica
47749		RX	PXLB	CD	Atlantic College
47750	a	RX	PXLB	CD	Royal Mail Cheltenham
47756		RX	PXLB	CD	Royal Mail Tyneside
47757	a	RX	PXLB	CD	Restitution
47758		RX	PXLB	CD	
47759		RX	PXLB	CD	
47760		RX	PXLB	CD	Restless
47761		RX	PXLB	CD	
47762		RX	PXLB	CD	
47763		RX	PXLB	CD	
47764		RX	PXLB	CD	Resounding
47765		RX	PXLB	CD	Ressaldar
47766		RX	PXLB	CD	Resolute
47767		RX	PXLB	CD	Saint Columba
47768		RX	PXLB	CD	Resonant
47769		RX	PXLB	CD	Resolve
47770		RX	PXLB	CD	Reserved
47771		RX	PXLB	CD	Heaton Traincare Depot
47772		RX	PXLB	CD	
47773		RX	PXLB	CD	Reservist
47774		RX	PXLB	CD	Poste Restante

PLATFORM 5 PUBLISHING LIMITED
MAIL ORDER LIST

NEW TITLES

BR Pocket Book No.1: Locomotives 39th edition Summer/Autumn 1997	£2.50
European Handbook No. 5: Swiss Railways 2nd edition	£13.50
Rails in the Isle of Wight (Midland)	£16.99
The Toy & Model Bus Handbook 1 - Early Diecast Models (British Bus)	£9.95
The Scottish Bus Handbook (British Bus)	£12.50
Bus Review 12 (Bus Enthusiast)	£7.50
Signalling Atlas and Signal Box Directory Great Britain & Ireland (Kay)	£9.95
The Midland's Settle & Carlisle Distance Diagrams (CRA)	£3.50
World Metro Systems 2nd edition (Capital)	£10.95
Moscow Railway Map (Quail)	£2.20
Albanian Railway Guide (Quail)	£1.20
Adelaide Track Maps (Quail)	£1.20
Korea Railway Map (Quail)	£2.00
Modern Traction Calendar 1998 (Rail Photoprints)	£4.50
Steam Traction Calendar 1998 (Rail Photoprints)	£4.50

MODERN BRITISH RAILWAY TITLES

British Railways Locomotives & Coaching Stock 1997	£9.95
BR Pocket Book No.2: Coaching Stock	£2.50
BR Pocket Book No.3: DMUs & Light Rail Systems	£2.50
BR Pocket Book No.4: Electric Multiple Units	£2.50
Preserved Locomotives of British Railways 9th edition	£7.95
Preserved Coaching Stock Part 1: BR Design Stock	£7.95
Preserved Coaching Stock Part 2: Pre-Nationalisation Stock	£8.95
Diesel & Electric Loco Register 3rd edition	£7.95
Valley Lines - The People's Railway	£9.95
Air Braked Series Wagon Fleet (SCTP)	£7.95
Departmental Coaching Stock 5th edition (SCTP)	£6.95
On-Track Plant on British Railways 5th edition (SCTP)	£7.95
Engineers Series Wagon Fleet 970000-999999 (SCTP)	£6.95
British Rail Wagon Fleet - B-Prefix Series (SCTP)	£6.95
British Rail Internal Users (SCTP)	£7.95
RIV Wagon Fleet (SCTP)	£5.95
Miles & Chains Volume 2 - London Midland (Milepost)	£1.95
Miles & Chains Volume 3 - Scottish (Milepost)	£1.95

Miles & Chains Volume 5 - Southern (Milepost) £1.95

OVERSEAS RAILWAYS

High Speed in Europe £9.95
High Speed in Japan £16.95
European Handbook No. 1: Benelux Railways 3rd edition £10.50
European Handbook No. 2: German Railways 3rd edition £12.50
European Handbook No. 3: Austrian Railways 3rd edition £10.50
European Handbook No. 6: Italian Railways 1st edition £13.50
European Handbook No. 7: Irish Railways 1st edition £9.95
Irish Railways In Colour: From Steam to Diesel 1955-1967 (Midland) £16.99
Irish Railways In Colour: A Second Glance 1947-1970 (Midland) £19.99
Irish Narrow Gauge - Pictorial History Part 1 (Midland) £15.99
Irish Narrow Gauge - Pictorial History Part 2 (Midland) £15.99
Locomotives & Railcars of Bord Na Mona (Midland) £4.99
The County Donegal Railway (Midland) £7.99
Midland & Great Western Railway of Ireland (Midland) £18.99
Railways of Southern Africa Loco Guide 1994 (Beyer-Garratt) £4.25

METRO SYSTEMS

The Twopenny Tube (Capital) [History of the Central Line] £5.95
Circles Under the Clyde (Capital) [Glasgow Subway] £15.95
Underground Official Handbook (Capital) £7.95
Docklands Light Rail Official Handbook (Capital) £7.95
Paris Metro Handbook (Capital) £7.95
The Berlin S-Bahn (Capital) £7.50
The Berlin U-Bahn (Capital) £7.50
Underground Architecture (Capital) £25.00
Mr Beck's Underground Map (Capital) £10.95

LIGHT RAIL TRANSIT & TRAMS

Tram to Supertram {Sheffield Trams] £4.95
Light Rail Review 3 .... £7.50
Light Rail Review 4 .... £7.50
Light Rail Review 5 .... £7.50
Light Rail Review 6 .... £7.50
Light Rail Review 7 .... £8.95
Manx Electric £8.95
Light Rail in Europe (Capital) £9.95
Tramway & Light Railway Atlas Germany 1996 (Blickpunkt Strassenbahn/LRTA) £10.45
The Tramways of Portugal (LRTA) £9.05

ATLASES, MAPS AND TRACK DIAGRAMS

Railway Track Diagrams No. 1: Scotland & Isle of Man (Quail) £6.50
British Rail Track Diagrams No. 4: Midland - 1990 Reprint (Quail) £6.95
British Rail Track Diagrams No. 5: Southern (Quail) £6.95
Railway Track Diagrams No. 6: Ireland (Quail) £5.50
London Transport Railway Track Map (Quail) £1.75
Czech Republic & Slovakia Railway Map (Quail) £1.70
Berlin Track Map (Quail) £2.20
Portugal Railway Map (Quail) £2.00
Greece Railway Map (Quail) £1.70
Poland Railway Map (Quail) £2.00
New York Railway Map (Quail) £1.70
Estonia Railway Map (Quail) £1.20
Latvia & Lithuania Railway Map (Quail) £2.00
Ukraine Belarus & Moldova Railway Atlas (Quail) £7.95
European Railway Atlas: France, Benelux (Ian Allan) £10.99
European Railway Atlas: Spain, Portugal, Italy, Greece (Ian Allan) £10.99
Track Diagram - South Yorkshire Supertram (HRT Rail Sales) £1.50
Track Diagram - Blackpool & Fleetwood (HRT Rail Sales) £1.00
Track Diagram - Tyne & Wear (HRT Rail Sales) £2.00

HISTORICAL RAILWAY TITLES

6203 'Princess Margaret Rose' £19.95
Steam Days on BR 1 - The Midland Line in Sheffield £4.95
Rails along the Sea Wall [Dawlish-Teignmouth Pictorial] £4.95
The Rolling Rivers £6.95
British Baltic Tanks £6.95
London Tilbury & Southend Railway Part 1 (Kay) £9.95
Bradshaw's Guide 1850 (Kay) £7.95
Railway Signal Engineering - Mechanical (Kay) £12.50
Railway Carriages & Wagons (Kay) £8.95

RAMBLING

Rambles by Rail 2 - Liskeard-Looe £1.95
Rambles by Rail 4 - The New Forest £1.95
Buxton Spa Line Rail Rambles £1.20

POSTCARDS

Sheffield Supertram - Car No. 12 crossing bridge over Sheffield Canal £0.30
Manchester Metrolink - Car No. 1021 in Aytoun Street £0.30

Quantity	Title		Price	Total
			SUB-TOTAL	
	Postage & Packing (see below for details)			
		TOTAL REMITTANCE		

Name: ....

Address: ....

.... Postcode: ....

Telephone No.: .... (Home) .... (Work)

Payment (Delete as appropriate)

I enclose my cheque (drawn on a UK bank)/postal order for £ . . . . payable to **'PLATFORM 5 PUBLISHING LTD'.**

Please debit my Visa/Access/Delta/Mastercard/Eurocard for £ . . . .

Card No: .... Card Expiry Date : ....

Signature: .... Date ....

Minimum credit card order accepted - £3.00.

Please send your remittance to:

Platform 5 Mail Order Department (PB)
3 Wyvern House, Sark Road
SHEFFIELD, S2 4HG, ENGLAND

If paying by credit card we can accept payment by post, telephone on: +44 (0)114 255 2625 or by fax on: +44 (0)114 255 2471.

Postage & packing please add: 10% UK (2nd Class); 20% Europe (Airmail); 30% Rest of World (Airfreight); 50% Rest of World (Airmail). If p&p works out at less than 30p, then please send 30p, this is the minimum post and packing accepted.

Please note that we cannot accept foreign currency cheques.

NOTE. When ordering publications in conjunction with a **Today's Railways** subscription offer please add on post and packing **before** deducting the voucher. Vouchers may **not** be combined.

47775		RX	PXLB	CD	Respite
47776		RX	PXLB	CD	Respected
47777		RX	PXLB	CD	Restored
47778		RX	PXLB	CD	Irresistible
47779		RX	PXLB	CD	
47780		RX	PXLB	CD	
47781		RX	PXLB	CD	Isle of Iona
47782		RX	PXLB	CD	
47783		RX	PXLB	CD	Saint Peter
47784		RX	PXLB	CD	Condover Hall
47785		E	PXLB	CD	Fiona Castle
47786	a	E	PXLB	CD	Roy Castle OBE
47787		RX	PXLB	CD	Victim Support
47788	a	RX	PXLB	CD	Captain Peter Manisty RN
47789	a	RX	PXLB	CD	Lindisfarne
47790	a	RX	PXLB	CD	Saint David/Dewi Sant
47791	a	RX	PXLB	CD	VENICE SIMPLON ORIENT EXPRESS
47792		RX	PXLB	CD	Saint Cuthbert
47793		RX	PXLB	CD	Saint Augustine

Class 47/4 continued. RA6. Max. Speed 95 m.p.h.

47798	a	0	PXLP	CD	Prince William
47799	a	0	PXLP	CD	Prince Henry
47802	+	I	ENXX	SF (S)	
47803	+	0	ENXX	SF (S)	
47805	a+	I	ILRA	CD	
47806	a+	I	ILRA	CD	
47807	a+	PL	ILRA	CD	
47810	a+	I	ILRA	CD	PORTERBROOK
47811	a+	I	IWLX	LA	
47812	a+	I	ILRA	CD	
47813	a+	I	IWLX	LA	
47814	a+	V	ILRA	CD	Totnes Castle
47815	a+	I	IWLA	LA	
47816	a+	I	IWLA	LA	Bristol Bath Road Quality Approved
47817	a+	PL	ILRA	CD	
47818	a+	I	ILRA	CD	
47822	a+	I	ILRA	CD	
47825	a+	I	ILRA	CD	Thomas Telford
47826	a+	I	ILRA	CD	
47827	a+	I	ILRA	CD	
47828	a+	I	ILRA	CD	
47829	a+	I	ILRA	CD	
47830	a+	I	SBXL	ZC (U)	
47831	a+	I	ILRA	CD	Bolton Wanderer
47832	a+	I	IWLA	LA	
47839	a+	I	ILRA	CD	
47840	a+	I	ILRA	CD	NORTH STAR
47841	a+	I	ILRA	CD	The Institution of Mechanical Engineers

47843	a+	I	ILRA	CD	
47844	a+	V	ILRA	CD	
47845	a+	I	IWLX	LA	County of Kent
47846	a+	U	IWLA	LA	THOR
47847	a+	I	ILRA	CD	
47848	a+	I	ILRA	CD	
47849	a+	I	ILRA	CD	
47851	a+	I	ILRA	CD	
47853	a+	I	ILRA	CD	
47854	a+	I	ILRA	CD	Women's Royal Voluntary Service
47971	*	BR	PXLK	CD	Robin Hood
47972		CS	FDKI	IM	The Royal Army Ordnance Corps
47976	*	C	PXLK	CD	Aviemore Centre

Class 47/3 continued. RA6. Max. Speed 75 m.p.h.

47981	C	ENRN	TO

CLASS 55　　　　　DELTIC　　　Co–Co

Built: 1961 by English Electric at Vulcan Foundry, Newton-le-Willows.
Engine: Two Napier-Deltic T18-25 of 1230 kW (1650 h.p.) at 1500 r.p.m.
Main Generators: Two English Electric EE829.
Traction Motors: EE538 axle-hung.
Max. Tractive Effort: 222 kN (50000 lbf).
Cont. Tractive Effort: 136 kN (30500 lbf) at 32.5 m.p.h.
Power At Rail: 1969 kW (2640 hp). **Length over Buffers:** 17.65 m.
Brake Force: 51 t. **Wheel Diameter:** 1092 mm.
Design Speed: 100 m.p.h. **Weight:** 105 t.
Max. Speed: 90 m.p.h. **RA:** 5.
Train Brakes: Air & vacuum. **Multiple Working:** Not equipped.
ETH Index: 66.

Ownership:
Owned by 9000 Locomotives Ltd.

55022	G	MBDL	SL	ROYAL SCOTS GREY

CLASS 56　　　BRUSH TYPE 5　　　Co–Co

Built: 1976–84 by Electroputere at Craiova, Romania (as sub contractors for Brush) or BREL at Doncaster or Crewe Works.
Engine: Ruston Paxman 16RK3CT of 2460 kW (3250 hp) at 900 rpm.
Main Alternator: Brush BA1101A.
Traction Motors: Brush TM73-62.
Max. Tractive Effort: 275 kN (61800 lbf).
Cont. Tractive Effort: 240 kN (53950 lbf) at 16.8 m.p.h.
Power At Rail: 1790 kW (2400 hp). **Length over Buffers:** 19.36 m.
Brake Force: 60 t. **Wheel Diameter:** 1143 mm.
Design Speed: 80 m.p.h. **Weight:** 125 t.
Max. Speed: 80 m.p.h. **RA:** 7.
Train Brakes: Air.

Multiple Working: Red Diamond coupling code.
All equipped with slow speed control.

56003	LH	FDBI	IM
56004		FDBI	IM
56006	LH	FDBI	IM	Ferrybridge 'C' Power Station
56007	FT	FDBI	IM
56008		FDYX	IM (U)
56010	FT	LNBK	CF
56011	F	FDBI	IM
56012	FC	FDYX	IM (U)
56014	FC	FDYX	IM (U)
56018	FT	LNBK	CF
56019	FR	LCWX	CF (U)
56021	LH	FDBI	IM
56022	FT	FDBI	IM
56025	FT	FDBI	IM
56027	LH	FDBI	IM
56029	F	FDBI	IM
56031	C	FDBI	IM
56032	E	LNBK	CF	Sir De Morgannwg/ County of South Glamorgan
56033	FT	FDBI	IM	Shotton Paper Mill
56034	LH	FDBI	IM	Castell Ogwr/Ogmore Castle
56035	LH	FDBI	IM
56036	CT	FDBI	IM
56037	E	LNBK	CF	Richard Trevithick
56038	FT	FDBI	IM	Western Mail
56039	LH	FDBI	IM	ABP Port of Hull
56040	FT	LNBK	CF	Oystermouth
56041	E	FDBI	IM
56043	FS	FDBI	IM
56044	FT	LNBK	CF	Cardiff Canton Quality Assured
56045	LH	FDBI	IM	British Steel Shelton
56046	C	FDBI	IM
56047	CT	FDBI	IM
56048	C	FDBI	IM
56049	CT	FDBI	IM
56050	LH	LGAM	ML	British Steel Teeside
56051	E	FDBI	IM
56052	FT	LNBK	CF	The Cardiff Rod Mill
56053	FT	LNBK	CF	Sir Morgannwg Ganol/ County of Mid Glamorgan
56054	FT	FDBI	IM	British Steel Llanwern
56055	LH	FDBI	IM
56056	FT	LGAM	ML
56057	E	LGAM	ML	British Fuels
56058	E	LGAM	ML
56059	E	FDBI	IM
56060	FT	LCWX	CF (U)
56061	FS	FDYX	IM (U)

56062	F	FDBI	IM	Mountsorrel
56063	F	FDBI	IM	Bardon Hill
56064	FT	LNBK	CF	
56065	E	FDBI	IM	
56066	FT	FDBI	IM	
56067	E	FDBI	IM	
56068	U	FDBI	IM	
56069	FS	FDBI	IM	Thornaby TMD
56070	FT	FDBI	IM	
56071	FT	FDBI	IM	
56072	FT	LGAM	ML	
56073	FT	LNBK	CF	
56074	LH	FDBI	IM	Kellingley Colliery
56075	F	FDBI	IM	West Yorkshire Enterprise
56076	FS	LNBK	CF	
56077	LH	FDBI	IM	Thorpe Marsh Power Station
56078	F	FDBI	IM	
56079	FT	LGAM	ML	
56080	F	FDBI	IM	Selby Coalfield
56081	F	FDBI	IM	
56082	F	FDBI	IM	
56083	LH	FDBI	IM	
56084	LH	FDBI	IM	
56085	LH	FDBI	IM	
56086	FT	FDBI	IM	The Magistrates' Association
56087	E	FDBI	IM	
56088	E	FDBI	IM	
56089	E	FDBI	IM	
56090	LH	FDBI	IM	
56091	F	FDBI	IM	Castle Donington Power Station
56092	FT	FDBI	IM	
56093	FT	FDBI	IM	The Institution of Mining Engineers
56094	FC	FDBI	IM	Eggborough Power Station
56095	F	FDBI	IM	Harworth Colliery
56096	E	FDBI	IM	
56097	FS	FDBI	IM	
56098	F	FDBI	IM	
56099	FT	FDBI	IM	Fiddlers Ferry Power Station
56100	LH	FDBI	IM	
56101	FT	FDBI	IM	Mutual Improvement
56102	LH	FDBI	IM	
56103	E	LNBK	CF	
56104	FC	LGAM	ML	
56105	E	FDBI	IM	
56106	LH	FDBI	IM	
56107	LH	FDBI	IM	
56108	F	FDBI	IM	
56109	LH	FDBI	IM	
56110	LH	FDBI	IM	Croft
56111	LH	FDBI	IM	
56112	LH	FDBI	IM	Stainless Pioneer

56113	FT	LNBK	CF	
56114	E	FDBI	IM	Maltby Colliery
56115	FT	LNBK	CF	
56116	LH	FDBI	IM	
56117	E	FDBI	IM	
56118	LH	FDBI	IM	
56119	FT	LNBK	CF	
56120	E	FDBI	IM	
56121	FC	LNBK	CF	
56123	FT	LGAM	ML	Drax Power Station
56124	FC	LGAM	ML	
56125	FT	FDBI	IM	
56126	FC	FDBI	IM	
56127	FT	FDBI	IM	
56128	FT	LGAM	ML	
56129	FT	LGAM	ML	
56130	LH	FDBI	IM	Wardley Opencast
56131	F	FDBI	IM	Ellington Colliery
56132	FT	FDBI	IM	
56133	FT	FDBI	IM	Crewe Locomotive Works
56134	FC	FDBI	IM	Blyth Power
56135	F	FDBI	IM	Port of Tyne Authority

CLASS 58　　　　BREL TYPE 5　　　Co–Co

Built: 1983–87 by BREL at Doncaster Works.
Engine: Ruston Paxman RK3ACT of 2460 kW (3300 hp) at 1000 rpm.
Main Alternator: Brush BA1101B.
Traction Motors: Brush TM73-62.
Max. Tractive Effort: 275 kN (61800 lbf).
Cont. Tractive Effort: 240 kN (53950 lbf) at 17.4 m.p.h.
Power At Rail: 1780 kW (2387 hp). 　**Length over Buffers:** 19.13 m.
Brake Force: 62 t. 　**Wheel Diameter:** 1120 mm.
Design Speed: 80 m.p.h. 　**Weight:** 130 t.
Max. Speed: 80 m.p.h. 　**RA:** 7.
Train Brakes: Air.
Multiple Working: Red Diamond coupling code.
All equipped with slow speed control.

58001	FM	ENBN	TO	
58002	ML	ENBN	TO	Daw Mill Colliery
58003	FM	ENBN	TO	Markham Colliery
58004	FM	ENBN	TO	
58005	ML	ENBN	TO	Ironbridge Power Station
58006	F	ENBN	TO	
58007	FM	ENBN	TO	Drakelow Power Station
58008	ML	ENBN	TO	
58009	FM	ENBN	TO	
58010	FM	ENBN	TO	
58011	FM	ENBN	TO	Worksop Depot
58012	FM	ENBN	TO	

58013	ML	ENBN	TO	
58014	ML	ENBN	TO	Didcot Power Station
58015	FM	ENBN	TO	
58016	E	ENBN	TO	
58017	FM	ENBN	TO	Eastleigh Depot
58018	FM	ENBN	TO	High Marnham Power Station
58019	FM	ENBN	TO	Shirebrook Colliery
58020	FM	ENBN	TO	Doncaster Works
58021	ML	ENBN	TO	Hither Green Depot
58022	FM	ENBN	TO	
58023	ML	ENBN	TO	Peterborough Depot
58024	E	ENBN	TO	
58025	E	ENBN	TO	
58026	FM	ENBN	TO	
58027	FM	ENBN	TO	
58028	FM	ENBN	TO	
58029	FM	ENBN	TO	
58030	E	ENBN	TO	
58031	FM	ENBN	TO	
58032	ML	ENBN	TO	Thoresby Colliery
58033	E	ENBN	TO	
58034	FM	ENBN	TO	Bassetlaw
58035	FM	ENBN	TO	
58036	ML	ENBN	TO	
58037	E	ENBN	TO	
58038	ML	ENBN	TO	
58039	E	ENBN	TO	
58040	FM	ENBN	TO	Cottam Power Station
58041	FM	ENBN	TO	Ratcliffe Power Station
58042	ML	ENBN	TO	Petrolea
58043	FM	ENBN	TO	
58044	FM	ENBN	TO	Oxcroft Opencast
58045	FM	ENBN	TO	
58046	ML	ENBN	TO	Asfordby Mine
58047	E	ENBN	TO	Manton Colliery
58048	E	ENBN	TO	
58049	E	ENBN	TO	Littleton Colliery
58050	ML	ENBN	TO	Toton Traction Depot

CLASS 59   GENERAL MOTORS TYPE 5   Co–Co

Built: 1985 (59001–4), 1989 (59005) by General Motors, La Grange, Illinois, U.S.A. or 1990 (59101–4), 1994 (59201) and 1995 (59202–6) by General Motors, London, Ontario, Canada.
Engine: General Motors 645E3C two stroke of 2460 kW (3300 hp) at 900 rpm.
Main Alternator: General Motors AR11 MLD-D14A.
Traction Motors: General Motors D77B.
Max. Tractive Effort: 506 kN (113 550 lbf).
Cont. Tractive Effort: 291 kN (65 300 lbf) at 14.3 m.p.h.
Power At Rail: 1889 kW (2533 hp).   **Length over Buffers:** 21.35 m.

Brake Force: 69 t.   **Wheel Diameter:** 1067 mm.
Weight: 121 t.   **RA:** 7.
Design Speed: 60 m.p.h. (75 m.p.h. Class 59/2).
Max. Speed: 60 m.p.h. (75 m.p.h. Class 59/2).

Class 59/0. Owned by Foster-Yeoman Ltd.

Non-standard livery:
Blue/silver/blue livery with white lettering and cast numberplates.

59001	**O**	XYPO	MD	YEOMAN ENDEAVOUR
59002	**O**	XYPO	MD	ALAN J DAY
59004	**O**	XYPO	MD	PAUL A HAMMOND
59005	**O**	XYPO	MD	KENNETH J. PAINTER

Class 59/1. Owned by ARC Limited.

Non-standard livery:
Yellow/grey with grey lettering and cast numberplates.

59101	**O**	XYPA	WH	Village of Whatley
59102	**O**	XYPA	WH	Village of Chantry
59103	**O**	XYPA	WH	Village of Mells
59104	**O**	XYPA	WH	Village of Great Elm

Class 59/2. Owned by National Power.

Non-standard livery:
Grey/red/white and blue with white and red lettering and cast numberplates.

59201	**O**	XYPN	FB	Vale of York
59202	**O**	XYPN	FB	Vale of White Horse
59203	**O**	XYPN	FB	Vale of Pickering
59204	**O**	XYPN	FB	Vale of Glamorgan
59205	**O**	XYPN	FB	Vale of Evesham
59206	**O**	XYPN	FB	Pride of Ferrybridge

CLASS 60   BRUSH TYPE 5   Co–Co

Built: 1989–1993 by Brush Traction at Loughborough.
Engine: Mirrlees MB275T of 2310 kW (3100 hp) at 1000 rpm.
Main Alternator: Brush .
Traction Motors: Brush separately excited.
Max. Tractive Effort: 500 kN (106500 lbf).
Cont. Tractive Effort: 336 kN (71570 lbf) at 17.4 m.p.h.
Power At Rail: 1800 kW (2415 hp).   **Length over Buffers:** 21.34 m.
Brake Force: 74 t.   **Wheel Diameter:** 1118 mm.
Design Speed: 62 m.p.h.   **Weight:** 129 t.
Max. Speed: 60 m.p.h.   **RA:** 7.
Multiple Working: Within class.
All equipped with slow speed control.

60001		**E**	ENAN	TO	
60002	+	**E**	FDAI	IM	
60003		**E**	FDAI	IM	FREIGHT TRANSPORT ASSOCIATION

60004	+	E	FDAI	IM	
60005		FT	ENAN	TO	Skiddaw
60006		FM	ENAN	TO	
60007	+	LH	FDAI	IM	
60008		LH	FDAI	IM	GYPSUM QUEEN II
60009	+	E	LNAK	CF	
60010		E	ENAN	TO	
60011		ML	ENAN	TO	
60012	+	E	LNAK	CF	
60013		F	ENAN	TO	Robert Boyle
60014		E	ENAN	TO	
60015	+	FT	LNAK	CF	Bow Fell
60016		E	LNAK	CF	
60017	+	E	LNAK	CF	Shotton Works Centenary Year 1996
60018		E	ENAN	TO	
60019		E	ENAN	TO	
60020	+	E	FDAI	IM	
60021	+	F	FDAI	IM	Pen-y-Ghent
60022	+	E	ENAN	TO	
60023		E	FDAI	IM	
60024		E	FDAI	IM	
60025	+	LH	FDAI	IM	
60026	+	E	FDAI	IM	
60027	+	E	FDAI	IM	
60028	+	E	FDAI	IM	
60029		FT	ENAN	TO	Ben Nevis
60030		E	FDAI	IM	
60031		FS	FDAI	IM	Ben Lui
60032		FT	ENAN	TO	William Booth
60033		FT	ENAN	TO	
60034		FT	LNAK	CF	Carnedd Llewelyn
60035		FT	LNAK	CF	Florence Nightingale
60036		FT	ENAN	TO	Sgurr Na Ciche
60037		E	LNAK	CF	Aberddawan/Aberthaw
60038	+	LH	FDAI	IM	
60039		E	ENAN	TO	
60040		E	ENAN	TO	
60041	+	E	LNAK	CF	
60042		E	ENAN	TO	
60043		E	ENAN	TO	
60044		ML	ENAN	TO	Ailsa Craig
60045		F	ENAN	TO	Josephine Butler
60046		F	ENAN	TO	William Wilberforce
60047	+	E	ENAN	TO	
60048		E	ENAN	TO	
60049		E	FDAI	IM	
60050		E	FDAI	IM	
60051		E	FDAI	IM	
60052		E	FDAI	IM	
60053		E	FDAI	IM	Nordic Terminal
60054	+	FP	FDAI	IM	Charles Babbage

60055		FT	·ENAN	TO	Thomas Barnardo
60056		FT	ENAN	TO	William Beveridge
60057		FC	ENAN	TO	Adam Smith
60058		FT	ENAN	TO	John Howard
60059	+	LH	FDAI	IM	Swinden Dalesman
60060		FC	ENAN	TO	James Watt
60061		FT	ENAN	TO	Alexander Graham Bell
60062		FT	LNAK	CF	Samuel Johnson
60063		FT	LNAK	CF	James Murray
60064	+	FL	FDAI	IM	Back Tor
60065		FT	ENAN	TO	Kinder Low
60066		FT	ENAN	TO	John Logie Baird
60067		F	FDAI	IM	James Clerk-Maxwell
60068		F	FDAI	IM	Charles Darwin
60069		F	FDAI	IM	Humphry Davy
60070	+	FL	FDAI	IM	John Loudon McAdam
60071	+	FM	ENAN	TO	Dorothy Garrod
60072		FM	ENAN	TO	Cairn Toul
60073		FM	ENAN	TO	
60074		FM	ENAN	TO	Braeriach
60075		FM	ENAN	TO	
60076		FM	ENAN	TO	
60077	+	FM	ENAN	TO	Canisp
60078		ML	ENAN	TO	
60079		FM	ENAN	TO	Foinaven
60080	+	FT	LNAK	CF	Kinder Scout
60081		FT	LNAK	CF	
60082		FA	FDAI	IM	Mam Tor
60083		E	ENAN	TO	
60084		FT	LNAK	CF	Cross Fell
60085		FT	ENAN	TO	
60086		FM	ENAN	TO	Schiehallion
60087		FM	ENAN	TO	Slioch
60088		FM	ENAN	TO	Buachaille Etive Mor
60089		FT	LNAK	CF	Arcuil
60090	+	FC	FDAI	IM	Quinag
60091		FC	FDAI	IM	An Teallach
60092		FT	ENAN	TO	Reginald Munns
60093		FT	LNAK	CF	Jack Stirk
60094		FM	ENAN	TO	Tryfan
60095		F	ENAN	TO	
60096		FT	LNAK	CF	Ben Macdui
60097		FT	ENAN	TO	Pillar
60098		E	ENAN	TO	Charles Francis Brush
60099		FM	ENAN	TO	Ben More Assynt
60100		FM	ENAN	TO	Boar of Badenoch

2. ELECTRIC LOCOMOTIVES

CLASS 71   BR DESIGN   Bo–Bo

Built: 1958–60 by BR at Doncaster Works
Supply System: 660–850 V d.c. from third rail or overhead supply.
Traction Motors:
Max. Tractive Effort: 191kN (43000 lbf).
Continuous Rating: 1715 kW (2300 hp).
Cont. Tractive Effort: 55kN (12400 lbf) at 69.6 m.p.h.
Maximum Rail Power:

Brake Force: 68 t.	**Length over Buffers:** m.
Design Speed: m.p.h.	**Weight:** 77 t.
Max. Speed: 90 m.p.h.	**RA:** 9.
Wheel Diameter: 1219 mm.	**ETH Index:**

Train Brakes: Air, Vacuum and electro-pneumatic.
Multiple Working: With Class 33/1, Class 73 and various 750 V d.c. EMUs.
Coupling: Drop-head buckeye.

Ownership:
Part of the National Collection.

Carries original number E 5001.

71001   **G**   MBEL   SE

CLASS 73/0   ELECTRO-DIESEL   Bo–Bo

Built: 1962 by BR at Eastleigh Works.
Supply System: 660–850 V d.c. from third rail.
Engine: English Electric 4SRKT of 447 kW (600 hp) at 850 rpm.
Main Generator: English Electric 824/3D.
Traction Motors: English Electric 542A.
Max. Tractive Effort: Electric 187 kN (42000 lbf). Diesel 152 kN (34100 lbf).
Continuous Rating: Electric 1060 kW (1420 hp) giving a tractive effort of 43 kN (9600 lbf) at 55.5 m.p.h.
Cont. Tractive Effort: Diesel 72 kN (16100 lbf) at 10 m.p.h.
Maximum Rail Power: Electric 1830 kW (2450 hp) at 37 m.p.h.

Brake Force: 31 t.	**Length over Buffers:** 16.36 m.
Design Speed: 80 m.p.h.	**Weight:** 76.5 t.
Max. Speed: 60 m.p.h.	**RA:** 6.
Wheel Diameter: 1016 mm.	**ETH Index (Elec. power):** 66.

Train Brakes: Air, Vacuum and electro-pneumatic.
Multiple Working: Within sub-class, with Class 33/1, Class 71 and various 750 V d.c. EMUs.
Couplings: Drop-head buckeye.

Formerly numbered E 6002/5.

73002	**BR**	HEBD	BD (U)
73005		HEBD	BD

CLASS 73/1 & 73/2 ELECTRO–DIESEL Bo–Bo

Built: 1965–67 by English Electric Co. at Vulcan Foundry, Newton le Willows.
Supply System: 660–850 V d.c. from third rail.
Engine: English Electric 4SRKT of 447 kW (600 hp) at 850 rpm.
Main Generator: English Electric 824/5D.
Traction Motors: English Electric 546/1B.
Max. Tractive Effort: Electric 179 kN (40000 lbf). Diesel 160 kN (36000 lbf).
Continuous Rating: Electric 1060 kW (1420 hp) giving a tractive effort of 35 kN (7800 lbf) at 68 m.p.h.
Cont. Tractive Effort: Diesel 60 kN (13600 lbf) at 11.5 m.p.h.
Maximum Rail Power: Electric 2350 kW (3150 hp) at 42 m.p.h.
Brake Force: 31 t.   **Length over Buffers:** 16.36 m.
Design Speed: 90 m.p.h.   **Weight:** 77 t.
Max. Speed: 60 (90*) m.p.h.   **RA:** 6.
Wheel Diameter: 1016 mm.   **ETH Index (Elec. power):** 66.
Train Brakes: Air, Vacuum and electro-pneumatic.
Multiple Working: Within sub-class, with Class 33/1, Class 71 and various 750 V d.c. EMUs.
Couplings: Drop-head buckeye.

Ownership:
All Gatwick Express locos are owned by Porterbrook Leasing Company.

Non-standard Livery:
73101 is Pullman umber & cream.

a Vacuum brake isolated.

Formerly numbered E 6001–20/22–26/28–49 (not in order).

73101		**0**	EWEB	EH	The Royal Alex'
73103		**I0**	EWEB	EH	
73104		**I0**	EWEB	EH	
73105		**C**	EWEB	EH	
73106		**D**	EWEB	EH	
73107		**C**	EWEB	EH	Redhill 1844–1994
73108		**C**	EWEB	EH	
73109	*	**SC**	HYSB	BM	Battle of Britain 50th Anniversary
73110		**C**	EWEB	EH	
73114		**ML**	EWEB	EH	Stewarts Lane Traction Maintenance Depot
73117		**I0**	EWEB	EH	University of Surrey
73118	c	**EP**	GPSN	SL	
73119		**C**	EWEB	EH	Kentish Mercury
73126		**N**	ENXX	SL (U)	Kent & East Sussex Railway
73128		**E**	EWRB	EH	
73129		**N**	EWEB	EH	City of Winchester
73130	c	**EP**	GPSN	SL	
73131		**E**	EWRB	EH	
73132		**I0**	EWRB	EH	
73133		**ML**	EWEB	EH	The Bluebell Railway

73134	IO	EWEB	EH	Woking Homes 1885–1985
73136	ML	EWEB	EH	Kent Youth Music
73138	C	EWEB	EH	
73139	IO	EWRB	EH	
73140	IO	EWRB	EH	
73141	IO	EWRB	EH	
73201	a*	GX	IVGA	SL	Broadlands
73202	a*	GX	IVGA	SL	Royal Observer Corps
73203	a*	GX	IVGA	SL	
73204	a*	GX	IVGA	SL	Stewarts Lane 1860–1985
73205	a*	GX	IVGA	SL	
73206	a*	GX	IVGA	SL	Gatwick Express
73207	a*	GX	IVGA	SL	County of East Sussex
73208	a*	GX	IVGA	SL	Croydon 1883–1983
73209	a*	GX	IVGA	SL	
73210	a*	GX	IVGA	SL	Selhurst
73211	a*	GX	IVGA	SL	
73212	a*	GX	IVGA	SL	Airtour Suisse
73213	a*	GX	IVGA	SL	University of Kent at Canterbury
73235	a*	GX	IVGA	SL	

CLASS 73/9   ELECTRO–DIESEL   Bo–Bo

For details see Class 73/0. Sandite fitted locos.

Formerly numbered E 6001/6.

| 73901 | MD | HEBD | BD |
| 73906 | MD | HEBD | BD |

NOTES FOR CLASSES 86–91.

The following common features apply to all locos of Classes 86–91.

Supply System: 25 kV a.c. from overhead equipment.
Communication Equipment: Driver–guard telephone.
Multiple Working: Time division multiplex system.

a vacuum brake isolated.

Class 86 were formerly numbered E 3101–3200 (not in order).

CLASS 86/1   BR DESIGN   Bo–Bo

Built: 1965–66 by English Electric Co. at Vulcan Foundry, Newton le Willows or BR at Doncaster Works. Rebuilt with Class 87 type bogies and motors. Tap changer control.
Traction Motors: GEC G412AZ frame mounted.
Max. Tractive Effort: 258 kN (58000 lbf).
Continuous Rating: 3730 kW (5000 hp) giving a tractive effort of 95 kN (21300 lbf) at 87 m.p.h.
Maximum Rail Power: 5860 kW (7860 hp) at 50.8 m.p.h.

Brake Force: 40 t.
Design Speed: 110 m.p.h.
Max. Speed: 110 m.p.h.
ETH Index: 74.
Train Brakes: Air & Vacuum.
Length over Buffers: 17.83 m.
Weight: 87 t.
RA: 6.
Wheel Diameter: 1150 mm.
Electric Brake: Rheostatic.

Ownership:
Owned by Eversholt Train Leasing Company.

86101	I	SAXL	ZC (U)	Sir William A Stanier FRS
86102	a I	IWPA	WN	Robert A Riddles
86103	I	SAXL	ZC (U)	André Chapelon

CLASS 86/2   BR DESIGN   Bo–Bo

Built: 1965–66 by English Electric Co. at Vulcan Foundry, Newton le Willows or BR at Doncaster Works. Later rebuilt with resilient wheels and flexicoil suspension. Tap changer control.
Traction Motors: AEI 282BZ.
Max. Tractive Effort: 207 kN (46500 lbf).
Continuous Rating: 3010 kW (4040 hp) giving a tractive effort of 85 kN (19200 lbf) at 77.5 m.p.h.
Maximum Rail Power: 4550 kW (6100 hp) at 49.5 m.p.h.
Brake Force: 40 t.
Design Speed: 125 m.p.h.
Max. Speed: 100 (110§) m.p.h.
ETH Index: 74.
Train Brakes: Air & Vacuum.
Length over Buffers: 17.83 m.
Weight: 85 t–86 t.
RA: 6.
Wheel Diameter: 1156 mm.
Electric Brake: Rheostatic.

Ownership:
All Anglia Railways and Virgin locos are owned by Eversholt Train Leasing Company.

86204	I	ICCA	LG	City of Carlisle
86205	a I	ICCA	LG	City of Lancaster
86206	a I	ICCA	LG	City of Stoke on Trent
86207	a I	IWPA	WN	City of Lichfield
86208	a I	PXLE	CE	City of Chester
86209	a§ I	IWPA	WN	City of Coventry
86210	RX	PXLE	CE	C.I.T. 75th Anniversary
86212	I	ICCA	LG	Preston Guild 1328–1992
86213	I	ICCA	LG	Lancashire Witch
86214	I	ICCA	LG	Sans Pareil
86215	a I	IANA	NC	
86216	a I	SAXL	LG (S)	Meteor
86217	a I	IANA	NC	City University
86218	I	IANA	NC	YEAR OF OPERA & MUSICAL THEATRE 1997
86219	I	SAXL	ZH (U)	Phoenix
86220	a I	IANA	NC	The Round Tabler
86221	a I	IANA	NC	B.B.C. Look East
86222	I	ICCA	LG	Clothes Show Live
86223	a I	IANA	NC	Norwich Union

86224	a§	I	IWPA	WN	Caledonian
86225	a§	I	IWPA	WN	Hardwicke
86226		I	ICCA	LG	CHARLES RENNIE MACKINTOSH
86227	a	I	ICCA	LG	Sir Henry Johnson
86228		I	SAXL	CE (U)	Vulcan Heritage
86229	a	I	ICCA	LG	Sir John Betjeman
86230	a	I	IANA	NC	
86231	a§	I	IWPA	WN	Starlight Express
86232	a	I	IANA	NC	Norfolk and Norwich Festival
86233	a	I	ICCA	LG	Laurence Olivier
86234	a	I	ICCA	LG	J B Priestley OM
86235	a	I	IANA	NC	Crown Point
86236	a	I	IWPA	WN	Josiah Wedgwood MASTER POTTER 1736–1795
86237	a	I	IANA	NC	University of East Anglia
86238	a	I	IANA	NC	European Community
86240	a	I	IWPA	WN	Bishop Eric Treacy
86241		RX	PXLE	CE	Glenfiddich
86242		I	IWPA	WN	James Kennedy GC
86243		RX	PXLE	CE	
86244	a	I	ICCA	LG	The Royal British Legion
86245	a	I	IWPA	WN	Dudley Castle
86246	a	I	IANA	NC	Royal Anglian Regiment
86247	a	I	ICCA	LG	Abraham Darby
86248		I	IWPA	WN	Sir Clwyd/County of Clwyd
86249	a	I	SAXL	ZC (U)	County of Merseyside
86250	a	I	IANA	NC	The Glasgow Herald
86251		I	IWPA	WN	The Birmingham Post
86252	a	I	ICCA	LG	The Liverpool Daily Post
86253	a	I	IWPA	WN	The Manchester Guardian
86254		RX	PXLE	CE	
86255		I	ICCA	LG	Penrith Beacon
86256		I	IWPA	WN	Pebble Mill
86257	a	I	IANA	NC (U)	Snowdon
86258	a	I	IWPA	WN	Talyllyn–The First Preserved Railway
86259	a	I	ICCA	LG	Greater MANCHESTER THE LIFE & SOUL OF BRITAIN
86260	a	I	ICCA	LG	Driver Wallace Oakes G.C.
86261		E	PXLE	CE	THE RAIL CHARTER PARTNERSHIP

CLASS 86/4 & 86/6   BR DESIGN   Bo–Bo

Built: 1965–66 by English Electric Co. at Vulcan Foundry, Newton le Willows or BR at Doncaster Works. Later rebuilt with resilient wheels and flexicoil suspension. Tap changer control.
Traction Motors: AEI 282AZ.
Max. Tractive Effort: 258 kN (58000 lbf).
Continuous Rating: 2680 kW (3600 hp) giving a tractive effort of 89 kN (20000 lbf) at 67 m.p.h.
Maximum Rail Power: 4400 kW (5900 hp) at 38 m.p.h.

Brake Force: 40 t.
Design Speed: 100 m.p.h.
Max. Speed: 100 (75*) m.p.h.
ETH Index: 74.
Train Brakes: Air & Vacuum.

Length over Buffers: 17.83 m.
Weight: 83 t–84 t.
RA: 6.
Wheel Diameter: 1156 mm.
Electric Brake: Rheostatic.

Ownership:
Freightliner 1995 locos Nos. 86612–39 are owned by Porterbrook Leasing Company.

Class 86/6 have the ETH equipment isolated.

86401		**RX**	PXLE	CE
86602	a*	**F**	DFNC	CE
86603	a*	**FF**	DFNC	CE
86604	a*	**FF**	DFNC	CE
86605	a*	**FF**	DFNC	CE
86606	a*	**FF**	DFNC	CE
86607	a*	**FD**	DFNC	CE
86608	a*	**FE**	DFNC	CE
86609	a*	**FD**	DFNC	CE
86610	a*	**FD**	DFNC	CE
86611	a*	**FF**	DFNC	CE	Airey Neave
86612	a*	**FF**	DFNC	CE	Elizabeth Garrett Anderson
86613		**F**	DFNC	CE	County of Lancashire
86614	a*	**FF**	DFNC	CE	Frank Hornby
86615	a*	**F**	DFNC	CE	Rotary International
86416		**RX**	PXLE	CE	
86417		**RX**	PXLE	CE	
86618	a*	**FF**	DFNC	CE	
86419		**RX**	PXLE	CE	
86620	a*	**F**	DFNC	CE	
86621	a*	**F**	DFNC	CE	London School of Economics
86622	a*	**FF**	DFNC	CE	
86623	a*	**FF**	DFNC	CE	
86424		**RX**	PXLE	CE	
86425		**RX**	PXLE	CE	Saint Mungo
86426		**E**	PXLE	CE	
86627	a*	**F**	DFNC	CE	The Industrial Society
86628	a*	**FF**	DFNC	CE	Aldaniti
86430		**RX**	PXLE	CE	Saint Edmund
86631	a*	**F**	DFNC	CE	
86632	a*	**F**	DFNC	CE	Brookside
86633	a*	**F**	DFNC	CE	Wulfruna
86634	a*	**F**	DFNC	CE	University of London
86635	a*	**FD**	DFNC	CE	
86636	a*	**F**	DFNC	CE	
86637	a*	**FF**	DFNC	CE	
86638	a*	**FF**	DFNC	CE	
86639	a*	**FD**	DFNC	CE	

CLASS 87   BR DESIGN   Bo–Bo

Built: 1973–75 by BREL at Crewe Works.
Traction Motors: GEC G412AZ frame mounted (87/0), G412BZ (87/1).
Max. Tractive Effort: 258 kN (58000 lbf).
Continuous Rating: 3730 kW (5000 hp) giving a tractive effort of 95 kN (21300 lbf) at 87 m.p.h. (Class 87/0), 3620 kW (4850 hp) giving a tractive effort of 96 kN (21600 lbf) at 84 m.p.h. (Class 87/1).
Maximum Rail Power: 5860 kW (7860 hp) at 50.8 m.p.h.

Brake Force: 40 t.	**Length over Buffers:** 17.83 m.
Design Speed: 110 m.p.h.	**Weight:** 83.5 t.
Max. Speed: 110 m.p.h. (100*)	**RA:** 6.
ETH Index: 95 (75§)	**Wheel Diameter:** 1150 mm.
Train Brakes: Air.	**Electric Brake:** Rheostatic.

Ownership:
All Virgin locos are owned by Porterbrook Leasing Company.

Class 87/0. Standard Design. Tap Changer Control.

87001	I	IWCA	WN	Royal Scot
87002	I	IWCA	WN	Royal Sovereign
87003	I	IWCA	WN	Patriot
87004	I	IWCA	WN	Britannia
87005	I	IWCA	WN	City of London
87006	I	IWCA	WN	City of Glasgow
87007	I	IWCA	WN	City of Manchester
87008	I	IWCA	WN	City of Liverpool
87009	§ I	IWCA	WN	City of Birmingham
87010	I	IWCA	WN	King Arthur
87011	I	IWCA	WN	The Black Prince
87012	I	IWCA	WN	The Royal Bank of Scotland
87013	I	IWCA	WN	John O' Gaunt
87014	I	IWCA	WN	Knight of the Thistle
87015	I	IWCA	WN	Howard of Effingham
87016	I	IWCA	WN	Willesden Intercity Depot
87017	I	IWCA	WN	Iron Duke
87018	I	IWCA	WN	Lord Nelson
87019	I	IWCA	WN	Sir Winston Churchill
87020	I	IWCA	WN	North Briton
87021	I	IWCA	WN	Robert the Bruce
87022	I	IWCA	WN	Cock o' the North
87023	I	IWCA	WN	Velocity
87024	I	IWCA	WN	Lord of the Isles
87025	I	IWCA	WN	County of Cheshire
87026	I	IWCA	WN	Sir Richard Arkwright
87027	I	IWCA	WN	Wolf of Badenoch
87028	I	IWCA	WN	Lord President
87029	§ I	IWCA	WN	Earl Marischal
87030	I	IWCA	WN	Black Douglas
87031	I	IWCA	WN	Hal o' the Wynd
87032	I	IWCA	WN	Kenilworth

87033	I	IWCA	WN	Thane of Fife
87034	I	IWCA	WN	William Shakespeare
87035	I	IWCA	WN	Robert Burns

Class 87/1. Thyristor Control.

| 87101 | * | DAMC | CE | STEPHENSON |

CLASS 89 BRUSH DESIGN Co-Co

Built: 1987 by BREL at Crewe Works.
Traction Motors: Brush design frame mounted.
Max. Tractive Effort: 205 kN (46000 lbf).
Continuous Rating: 2390 kW (3200 hp) giving a tractive effort of 105 kN (23600 lbf) at 92 m.p.h.
Maximum Rail Power:
Brake Force: 40 t.
Design Speed: 125 m.p.h.
Max. Speed: 125 m.p.h.
ETH Index: 95.
Train Brakes: Air.
Couplings: Drop-head buckeye.
Length over Buffers: 18.80 m.
Weight: 104 t.
RA: 6.
Wheel Diameter: 1150 mm.
Electric Brake: Rheostatic.

Ownership:
Owned by Great North Eastern Railway Ltd.

| 89001 | **GN** | IECB | BN | |

CLASS 90 GEC DESIGN Bo-Bo

Built: 1987–90 by BREL at Crewe Works. Thyristor control.
Traction Motors: GEC G412CY separately excited frame mounted.
Max. Tractive Effort: 258 kN (58000 lbf).
Continuous Rating: 3730 kW (5000 hp) giving a tractive effort of 95 kN (21300 lbf) at 87 m.p.h.
Maximum Rail Power: 5860 kW (7860 hp) at 68.3 m.p.h.
Brake Force: 40 t.
Design Speed: 110 m.p.h.
Max. Speed: 110 (75*) m.p.h.
ETH Index: 95.
Train Brakes: Air.
Couplings: Drop-head buckeye (removed on Class 90/1).
Length over Buffers: 18.80 m.
Weight: 84.5 t.
RA: 7.
Wheel Diameter: 1156 mm.
Electric Brake: Rheostatic.

Ownership:
All Virgin and Freightliner 1995 locos are owned by Porterbrook Leasing Company.

Non-standard Liveries:
90128 is in SNCB/NMBS (Belgian Railways) electric loco livery.
90129 is in DB (German Federal Railways) 'neurot' (new red) livery.
90130 is in SNCF (French Railways) 'Sybic' livery.
90136 is in livery FE, but with full yellow ends and roof and red 'Railfreight Distribution' lettering.

Class 90/0. As built.

90001	I	IWCA	WN	BBC Midlands Today
90002	V	IWCA	WN	Mission:Impossible
90003	I	IWCA	WN	THE HERALD
90004	I	IWCA	WN	The D' Oyly Carte Opera Company
90005	I	IWCA	WN	Financial Times
90006	I	IWCA	WN	High Sheriff
90007	I	IWCA	WN	Lord Stamp
90008	I	IWCA	WN	The Birmingham Royal Ballet
90009	I	IWCA	WN	The Economist
90010	I	IWCA	WN	275 Railway Squadron (Volunteers)
90011	I	IWCA	WN	The Chartered Institute of Transport
90012	I	IWCA	WN	British Transport Police
90013	I	IWCA	WN	The Law Society
90014	V	IWCA	WN	
90015	V	IWCA	WN	
90016	RX	PXLE	CE	
90017	RX	PXLE	CE	Rail express systems Quality Assured
90018	RX	PXLE	CE	
90019	RX	PXLE	CE	Penny Black
90020	E	PXLE	CE	Sir Michael Heron
90021	FE	DAMC	CE	
90022	FE	DAMC	CE	Freightconnection
90023	FE	DAMC	CE	
90024	FE	DAMC	CE	

Class 90/1. ETH equipment isolated.

90125	*	FE	DAMC	CE	Crewe International
90126	*	FE	DAMC	CE	Electric Maintenance Depot
90127	*	FD	DAMC	CE	Allerton T&RS Depot Quality Approved
90128	*	0	DAMC	CE	Vrachtverbinding
90129	*	0	DAMC	CE	Frachtverbindungen
90130	*	0	DAMC	CE	Fretconnection
90131	*	FE	DAMC	CE	Intercontainer
90132	*	FE	DAMC	CE	Cerestar
90133	*	FE	DAMC	CE	
90134	*	FE	DAMC	CE	
90135	*	FE	DAMC	CE	Crewe Basford Hall
90136	*	0	DAMC	CE	
90137	*	F	DAMC	CE	
90138	*	FE	DAMC	CE	
90139	*	FD	DAMC	CE	
90140	*	FD	DAMC	CE	
90141	*	F	DFLC	CE	
90142	*	F	DFLC	CE	
90143	*	FF	DFLC	CE	Freightliner Coatbridge
90144	*	F	DFLC	CE	
90145	*	FF	DFLC	CE	
90146	*	FF	DFLC	CE	

90147	*	FF	DFLC	CE
90148	*	FF	DFLC	CE
90149	*	FF	DFLC	CE
90150	*	FF	DFLC	CE

CLASS 91   GEC DESIGN   Bo–Bo

Built: 1988–91 by BREL at Crewe Works. Thyristor control.
Traction Motors: GEC G426AZ.
Continuous Rating: 4540 kW (6090 hp).
Maximum Rail Power: 4700 kW (6300 hp).
Brake Force: 45 t.
Design Speed: 140 m.p.h.
Max. Speed: 140 m.p.h.
ETH Index: 95.
Train Brakes: Air.
Couplings: Drop-head buckeye.
Length over Buffers: 19.40 m.
Weight: 84 t.
RA: 7.
Wheel Diameter: 1000 mm.
Electric Brake: Rheostatic.

Ownership:
Owned by Eversholt Train Leasing Company.

91001	GN	IECA	BN	
91002	GN	IECA	BN	
91003	GN	IECA	BN	
91004	GN	IECA	BN	
91005	GN	IECA	BN	
91006	GN	IECA	BN	
91007	GN	IECA	BN	
91008	GN	IECA	BN	
91009	GN	IECA	BN	The Samaritans
91010	GN	IECA	BN	
91011	GN	IECA	BN	
91012	GN	IECA	BN	
91013	GN	IECA	BN	
91014	GN	IECA	BN	
91015	GN	IECA	BN	
91016	GN	IECA	BN	
91017	GN	IECA	BN	
91018	GN	IECA	BN	
91019	GN	IECA	BN	
91020	GN	IECA	BN	
91021	GN	IECA	BN	
91022	GN	IECA	BN	
91023	GN	IECA	BN	
91024	GN	IECA	BN	
91025	GN	IECA	BN	
91026	GN	IECA	BN	
91027	GN	IECA	BN	
91028	GN	IECA	BN	
91029	GN	IECA	BN	
91030	GN	IECA	BN	
91031	GN	IECA	BN	

CLASS 92   BRUSH DESIGN   Co-Co

Built: 1993–5 by Brush Traction at Loughborough. Thyristor control.
Supply System: 25 kV a.c. from overhead equipment and 750 V d.c. third rail.
Electrical equipment: ABB Transportation, Zürich, Switzerland.
Traction Motors: Brush design.
Max. Tractive Effort: 400 kN (90 000 lbf).
Continuous Rating at Motor Shaft: 5040 kW (6760 hp).
Maximum Rail Power (25 kV a.c.): 5000 kW (6700 hp).
Maximum Rail Power (750 V d.c.): 4000 kW (5360 hp).
Brake Force: t.   **Length over Buffers:** 21.34 m.
Design Speed: 140 km/h (87½ m.p.h.).   **Weight:** 126 t.
Max. Speed: 140 km/h (87½ m.p.h.).   **RA:** 8.
ETH Index: 108.   **Wheel Diameter:** 1160 mm.
Train Brakes: Air.
Electric Brake: Rheostatic & regenerative.
Multiple Working: Time division multiplex system.
Communication Equipment: Driver–guard telephone.
Cab Signalling: Fitted with TVM430 cab signalling for Channel Tunnel.

Ownership:
92006/10/4/8/23/8/33/8/43 are owned by SNCF.
92020/1/32/40/4–6 are owned by Eurostar (UK) Ltd.

92001	**EP**	DADC	CE	Victor Hugo
92002	**EP**	DADC	CE	H G Wells
92003	**EP**	DADC	CE	Beethoven
92004	**EP**	DADC	CE	Jane Austen
92005	**EP**	DAVC	CE	Mozart
92006	**EP**	DAVC	CE	Louis Armand
92007	**EP**	DAVC	CE	Schubert
92008	**EP**	DAVC	CE	Jules Verne
92009	**EP**	DAVC	CE	Elgar
92010	**EP**	DADC	CE	Molière
92011	**EP**	DADC	CE	Handel
92012	**EP**	DADC	CE	Thomas Hardy
92013	**EP**	DAEC	CE	Puccini
92014	**EP**	DAVC	CE	Emile Zola
92015	**EP**	DADC	CE	D H Lawrence
92016	**EP**	DADC	CE	Brahms
92017	**EP**	DAEC	CE	Shakespeare
92018	**EP**	DAVC	CE	Stendhal
92019	**EP**	DADC	CE	Wagner
92020	**EP**	DADC	CE	Milton
92021	**EP**	DAVC	CE	Purcell
92022	**EP**	DAEC	CE	Charles Dickens
92023	**EP**	DAVC	CE	Ravel
92024	**EP**	DAEC	CE	J S Bach
92025	**EP**	DAEC	CE	Oscar Wilde
92026	**EP**	DADC	CE	Britten
92027	**EP**	DAEC	CE	George Eliot

92028	**EP**	DAVC	CE	Saint Saëns
92029	**EP**	DAVC	CE	Dante
92030	**EP**	DADC	CE	Ashford
92031	**EP**	DADC	CE	
92032	**EP**	DAIC	CE	César Franck
92033	**EP**	DADC	CE	Berlioz
92034	**EP**	DAVC	CE	Kipling
92035	**EP**	DAVC	CE	Mendelssohn
92036	**EP**	DAVC	CE	Bertolt Brecht
92037	**EP**	DADC	CE	Sullivan
92038	**EP**	DADC	CE	Voltaire
92039	**EP**	DAEC	CE	Johann Strauss
92040	**EP**	DAEC	CE	Goethe
92041	**EP**	DAVC	CE	Vaughan Williams
92042	**EP**	DAVC	CE	Honegger
92043	**EP**	DAVC	CE	Debussy
92044	**EP**	DAVC	CE	Couperin
92045	**EP**	DAVC	CE	Chaucer
92046	**EP**	DAVC	CE	Sweelinck

3. SERVICE LOCOMOTIVES

CLASS 97/8   EE SHUNTER   0–6–0

For details see Class 09. Severn Tunnel emergency train locomotive.

Non-Standard Livery: BR blue with grey cab.

| 97806 | (09017) | x | **0** | LNCF | CF | Normally kept at Sudbrook |

PRESERVED LOCOMOTIVES OF BRITISH RAILWAYS 9th edition
by Peter Hall & Peter Fox.

The complete guide to all remaining ex-British Railways and constituent companies, steam, diesel & electric locomotives, and diesel & electric multiple units. Full details of numbers carried, names and locations are provided for each vehicle, plus a full list of preservation sites and industrial locations. 128 pages including 16 in colour. A5 size. Thread Sewn. £7.95.

This title is available from the Platform 5 Mail Order Department. To order, please see the centre pages of this book.

4. LOCOMOTIVES AWAITING DISPOSAL

03079		Sandown	31286		Bescot Yard
03179	**N**	Ryde T&RSMD	31289		Bescot Yard
08222		Old Oak Common TMD	31290	**C**	Toton Yard
08419		ADtranz Crewe Works	31296	**FA**	Crewe Carriage Shed
08473		Leicester LIP	31299	**FO**	Stratford TMD
08515		Gateshead WRD	31320		Stratford TMD
08562		Old Oak Common TMD	31402		Bescot Yard
08565		Motherwell TMD	31403		Toton Yard
08609		Willesden TMD	31413	**O**	ADtranz Doncaster Works
08618		Gateshead WRD	31428		Bescot Yard
08634		Stratford TMD	31442		Crewe Carriage Shed
08666		Allerton TMD	31460		Bescot Yard
08673	**IO**	Allerton TMD	31547	**C**	Toton Yard
08677		Willesden TMD	31553	**C**	Toton Yard
08733		Motherwell TMD	31569	**C**	Toton Yard
08755		Millerhill Wagon Works	33008	**G**	Stewarts Lane T&RSMD
08793	**O**	Aberdeen Guild St Yard	33038		Stratford TMD
08829		Toton TMD	33205	**FD**	Hither Green LIP
08855		Aberdeen Guild St Yard	37252	**FD**	Doncaster TMD
08880		Allerton TMD	45015		Toton TMD
08895		Margam WRD	47096		Tinsley TMD
08898		Bescot Yard	47102		Tinsley TMD
20073		Bescot Yard	47190	**FP**	Tinsley TMD
20113	**O**	Brush, Loughborough	47214	**FD**	Tinsley TMD
20119		Toton TMD	47249	**FR**	Tinsley TMD
20154		Toton TMD	47318	**FO**	Bescot Yard
20175	**O**	Brush, Loughborough	47321	**F**	Tinsley TMD
20177		Toton TMD	47325	**FO**	Tinsley TMD
25083		Crewe Carriage Shed	47515	**M**	Crewe Coal Siding
31105	**FT**	Bescot Yard	47707	**RX**	Crewe Basford Hall Yard
31112	**CT**	Bescot Yard	47714	**RX**	Crewe Basford Hall Yard
31168		Bescot Yard	47850	**I**	ADtranz Crewe Works
31180	**FR**	Toton Yard	56009	**FC**	Brush, Loughborough
31184	**FO**	Toton Yard	56013	**FC**	Toton TMD
31196	**C**	Stratford TMD	56023	**FC**	Toton TMD
31209	**FA**	Toton Yard	56028	**FC**	Margam WRD
31217	**FC**	Toton Yard	56030	**FC**	Margam WRD
31282	**FR**	Bescot Yard	56122	**FC**	Toton TMD
31283	**O**	Stratford TMD	97653	**O**	Reading T&RSMD

Non-standard Liveries:

08793 is in London & North Eastern Railway apple green.

20113 & 20175 are RFS grey with blue and yellow bodyside stripes and carry numbers 2003 and 2007 respectively.

31283 is BR blue with large numbers.

31413 is BR blue with yellow cabsides, a light blue stripe along the bottom of the body and a red band around the bottom of the cabs.

97653 is Departmental yellow.

▲ One of the two Class 47s recently repainted in EWS livery, Class 47 No. 47785 'Fiona Castle' pauses at Hereford on 13th June 1997 before leaving light engine for Birmingham New Street.　**Bob Sweet**

▼ Loadhaul liveried Class 56 No. 56116 is pictured near Bridgend on 28th May 1997 with the 11.40 Swansea–Newport 'Enterprise' service.　**Rodney Lissenden**

An Immingham to Scunthorpe coal train passes Melton Ross behind Transrail liveried Class 56 No. 56127 on 14th May 1997.

Ian A. Lyall

▲ A Crawley to Acton Yard stone train with ARC liveried Class 59 No. 59102 'Village of Chantry' in charge pauses at a signal on Acton Bank, West London. The date is 24th October 1995. **Kevin Conkey**

▼ EWS liveried Class 60 No. 60049 passes through the Tyne valley with 6M46, the Redcar–Hardendale lime hoppers on 29th March 1997. **Dave McAlone**

▲ Gatwick Express liveried Class 73 No. 73211 forks left after passing through Clapham Junction with the 13.30 London Victoria–Gatwick Airport on 8th February 1997. **Chris Wilson**

▼ A pair of Class 86/6s, both in Freightliner livery, Nos. 86618 & 86604 pass through Stratford on 20th March 1997 whilst working the 12.35 Tilbury–Crewe Freightliner service. **Rodney Lissenden**

▲ Intercity liveried Class 87 No. 87013 'John O'Gaunt' passes Lower Hatton, north Staffordshire on 20th May 1997 whilst working the 18.05 London Euston–Liverpool Lime Street service. The coaches are carrying the new Virgin Rail livery.
Hugh Ballantyne

▼ The recently reinstated Class 89 No. 89001 is pictured at London King's Cross on 24th May 1997, shortly before leaving with the 14.30 to Leeds. The loco now carries Great North Eastern Railway livery. **Peter Fox**

▲ Virgin Rail liveried Class 90 No. 90002 'Mission:Impossible' at Manchester Piccadilly on 10th March 1997. The train is the 11.30 to London Euston and the locomotive is at the south end of the train instead of the north as is usual.

Peter Fox

▼ Three light engines consisting of Class 90s Nos. 90134, in Railfreight Distribution livery, DB "new red" liveried No. 90129 'Frachtverbindungen' and Class 92 No. 92043 'Debussy' pass Slindon, Staffordshire heading for Crewe on 21st August 1996.

Hugh Ballantyne

All Class 91s now carry the new GNER blue livery. Here, No. 91007 approaches Hambleton Junction with a London King's Cross–Edinburgh train on 2nd June 1997.

Paul Senior

European Passenger Services liveried Class 92 No. 92037 'Sullivan' hauls the 09.33 Wembley–Dollands Moor freight through Swanley on 17th March 1997.
Rodney Lissenden

5. POOL CODES & ALLOCATIONS

SERCO

CDJD Derby Etches Park Class 08 (Research)

08417   08956

RAILFREIGHT DISTRIBUTION

DAAN Allerton Class 08

08569	08653 FE	08739	08799	08837 D	08856	08907 0
08939						

DADC Crewe Electric Class 92 (Dollands Moor–Wembley)

92001 EP	92002 EP	92003 EP	92004 EP	92010 EP	92011 EP	92012 EP
92015 EP	92016 EP	92019 EP	92020 EP	92026 EP	92030 EP	92031 EP
92033 EP	92037 EP	92038 EP				

DAEC Crewe Electric Class 92 (Non-Operational)

92013 EP	92017 EP	92022 EP	92024 EP	92025 EP	92027 EP	92039 EP
92040 EP						

DAET Tinsley Class 47

47033 FE	47049 FE	47051 FE	47053 FE	47085 FE	47095 FE	47125 FE
47145 0	47146 FE	47150 FE	47186 FE	47194 FD	47200 FE	47201 FE
47210 FD	47211 FD	47213 FD	47217 FE	47218 FE	47219 FE	47226 FD
47228 FE	47229 FE	47236 FE	47237 FE	47241 FE	47245 FE	47258 FE
47276 FD	47280 FD	47281 FD	47284 FD	47285 FE	47286 FE	47287 FE
47293 FE	47297 FE	47298 FD	47304 FD	47306 FE	47307 FE	47309 FD
47310 FE	47312 FE	47313 FE	47314 FE	47326 FE	47335 FD	47338 FE
47344 FE	47348 FE	47351 FE	47355 FD	47360 FE	47362 FD	47363 F
47365 FE	47375 FE	47379 F	47525 FE	47540 C		

DAIC Crewe Electric Class 92 (EPS Testing)

92032 EP

DAMC Crewe Electric Class 87/1 & 90

87101	90021 FE	90022 FE	90023 FE	90024 FE	90125 FE	90126 FE
90127 FD	90128 0	90129 0	90130 0	90131 FE	90132 FE	90133 FE
90134 FE	90135 FE	90136 0	90137 F	90138 FE	90139 FD	90140 FD

DASY Allerton/Tinsley Class 08 (Saltley)

08535 D   08946 FE   08951 D   09011 D

DATI Tinsley Class 08

08879 0

DAVC   Crewe Electric Class 92 (100 mph Maximum)

92005 **EP**   92006 **EP**   92007 **EP**   92008 **EP**   92009 **EP**   92014 **EP**   92018 **EP**
92021 **EP**   92023 **EP**   92028 **EP**   92029 **EP**   92034 **EP**   92035 **EP**   92036 **EP**
92041 **EP**   92042 **EP**   92043 **EP**   92044 **EP**   92045 **EP**   92046 **EP**

DAWE   Allerton Class 08 (Wembley/Dagenham/Southampton)

08389   08482 **D**   08694   08737 **FE**   08825   08844   08872 **D**
09021 **FE**

DAXT   Locomotives Awaiting Repair

47144 **FD**   47188 **FE**   47299 **FE**   47316 **FE**   47328 **FD**   47378 **FD**

DAYX   Stored Locomotives

08393 **D**   08413 **D**   08655 **F**   08661 **FE**   08703   08751 **FE**   08784
08842   08902   08905 **FE**   08913 **D**   08926   09022   47222 **FD**
47291 **FD**   47555 **FE**

FREIGHTLINER 1995

DFLC   Crewe Electric Class 90/1

90141 **F**   90142 **F**   90143 **FF**   90144 **F**   90145 **FF**   90146 **FF**   90147 **FF**
90148 **FF**   90149 **FF**   90150 **FF**

DFLM   Crewe Diesel Class 47 (Multiple Working Fitted)

47114 **0**   47152 **FF**   47204 **F**   47205 **FF**   47234 **FF**   47279 **FF**   47292 **FD**
47303 **FF**   47330 **FD**   47361 **FF**

DFLR   Crewe Diesel Class 47 (Resilience Pool)

47052 **FF**   47157 **FF**   47206 **FF**   47209 **FF**   47212 **FF**   47225 **FF**   47290 **FF**
47296 **FF**   47301 **FF**   47305 **FF**   47323 **FF**   47337 **FF**   47339 **FF**   47345 **FF**
47354 **FF**   47370 **FF**   47371 **FF**   47376 **FF**   47377 **FF**

DFLS   Allerton/Crewe Diesel/Eastleigh/Stratford/Tinsley Class 08

08077 **0**   08530 **D**   08531 **D**   08575 **BS**   08585   08624   08642 **0**
08691 **G**   08745 **FE**   08891

DFLT   Crewe Diesel Class 47

47060 **F**   47079 **FF**   47197 **FF**   47207 **F**   47231 **FF**   47283 **F**   47289 **FF**
47302 **FR**   47317 **F**   47349 **FF**   47358 **FF**

DFNC   Crewe Electric Class 86/6

86602 **F**   86603 **FF**   86604 **FF**   86605 **FF**   86606 **FF**   86607 **FD**   86608 **FE**
86609 **FD**   86610 **FD**   86611 **FF**   86612 **FF**   86613 **F**   86614 **FF**   86615 **F**
86618 **F**   86620 **F**   86621 **F**   86622 **FF**   86623 **FF**   86627 **F**   86628 **FF**
86631 **F**   86632 **F**   86633 **F**   86634 **F**   86635 **FD**   86636 **F**   86637 **FF**
86638 **FF**   86639 **FD**

DHLT   Crewe Diesel Class 47 (Holding Pool)

47142 **FR**	47147 **F**	47156 **FD**	47187 **F**	47270 **FF**	47322 **FR**	47340 **C**
47347 **F**	47350 **FO**	47356 **FO**	47367 **FR**	47473 **BR**		

EWS (FORMERLY MAINLINE)

ENAN   Toton Class 60

60001 **E**	60005 **FT**	60006 **FM**	60010 **E**	60011 **ML**	60013 **F**	60014 **E**
60018 **E**	60019 **E**	60022 **E**	60029 **FT**	60032 **FT**	60033 **FT**	60036 **FT**
60039 **E**	60040 **E**	60042 **E**	60043 **E**	60044 **ML**	60045 **F**	60046 **F**
60047 **E**	60048 **E**	60055 **FT**	60056 **FT**	60057 **FC**	60058 **FT**	60060 **FC**
60061 **FT**	60065 **FT**	60066 **FT**	60071 **FM**	60072 **FM**	60073 **FM**	60074 **FM**
60075 **FM**	60076 **FM**	60077 **FM**	60078 **ML**	60079 **FM**	60083 **E**	60085 **FT**
60086 **FM**	60087 **FM**	60088 **FM**	60092 **FT**	60094 **FM**	60095 **F**	60097 **FT**
60098 **E**	60099 **FM**	60100 **FM**				

ENBN   Toton Class 58

58001 **FM**	58002 **ML**	58003 **FM**	58004 **FM**	58005 **ML**	58006 **F**	58007 **FM**
58008 **ML**	58009 **FM**	58010 **FM**	58011 **FM**	58012 **FM**	58013 **ML**	58014 **ML**
58015 **FM**	58016 **E**	58017 **FM**	58018 **FM**	58019 **FM**	58020 **FM**	58021 **ML**
58022 **FM**	58023 **ML**	58024 **E**	58025 **E**	58026 **FM**	58027 **FM**	58028 **FM**
58029 **FM**	58030 **E**	58031 **FM**	58032 **FM**	58033 **E**	58034 **FM**	58035 **FM**
58036 **ML**	58037 **E**	58038 **ML**	58039 **E**	58040 **FM**	58041 **FM**	58042 **ML**
58043 **FM**	58044 **FM**	58045 **FM**	58046 **ML**	58047 **E**	58048 **E**	58049 **E**
58050 **ML**						

ENRN   Toton Class 47 (Restricted Use)

47004 **G**	47519 **G**	47702 **F**	47981 **C**

ENSN   Toton Class 08/09 (Toton/Peterborough)

08441	08492	08495	08516 **D**	08528 **D**	08529	08538 **D**
08567	08580	08714 **RX**	08865	08886 **E**	09201 **D**	

ENTN   Toton Class 31/37 (Infrastructure)

37010 **C**	37013 **ML**	37038 **C**	37042 **E**	37046 **C**	37051 **E**	37055 **ML**
37057 **E**	37065 **ML**	37071 **C**	37072 **D**	37079 **FD**	37097 **C**	37098 **C**
37114 **E**	37162 **D**	37185 **C**	37222 **FM**	37238 **F**	37244 **F**	37248 **ML**
37264 **C**	37376 **FC**	37431 **M**	37715 **FM**	37798 **ML**		

ENXX   Stored Locomotives

08449	08607	08723	08773	31116 **O**	31135 **C**	31149 **FR**
31165 **G**	31181 **C**	31186 **C**	31187 **C**	31191 **C**	31205 **FR**	31219 **C**
31230 **FO**	31247 **FR**	31250 **C**	31252 **FO**	31268 **C**	31271 **FA**	31276 **FC**
31294 **FA**	31531 **C**	31541 **C**	31549 **C**	31551 **C**	31552 **C**	31558 **C**
31459	31461 **D**	31563 **C**	37035 **C**	37048 **FM**	37092 **C**	37137 **FM**
37227 **FM**	37241 **F**	37278 **FC**	47223 **F**	47278 **FP**	47366 **C**	47368 **F**
47462 **R**	47484 **G**	47526 **BR**	47802 **I**	47803 **O**	73126 **N**	

ENZX   Locomotives For Withdrawal

08540 **D**

EWDB   Stewarts Lane/Stratford Class 33/37 (Infrastructure)

33019 **C**	33025 **C**	33026 **C**	33030 **C**	33046 **C**	33051	33116
33202 **C**	37023 **ML**	37037 **FM**	37047 **ML**	37054 **C**	37074 **ML**	37077 **ML**
37106 **C**	37109 **E**	37133 **C**	37140 **C**	37167 **ML**	37198 **ML**	37203 **ML**
37216 **ML**	37219 **ML**	37242 **ML**	37262 **D**	37274 **ML**	37371 **ML**	37375 **C**
37377 **C**	37379 **ML**	37405 **E**	37423 **FT**	37676 **F**	37679 **F**	37703 **E**
37705 **FM**	37709 **FM**	37711 **FS**	37800 **E**	37803 **ML**	37890 **FM**	37891 **FM**
37892 **FM**						

EWEB   Eastleigh Class 73 (Infrastructure)

73101 **O**	73103 **IO**	73104 **IO**	73105 **C**	73106 **D**	73107 **C**	73108 **C**
73110 **C**	73114 **ML**	73117 **IO**	73119 **C**	73129 **N**	73133 **ML**	73134 **IO**
73136 **ML**	73138 **C**					

EWEH   Eastleigh Class 08

08480 **G**   08600 **D**   08854   08933 **E**   08940

EWHG   Stewarts Lane Class 09

09003   09009 **E**   09019 **ML**   09024 **ML**

EWOC   Old Oak Common Class 08/09

08523 **ML**	08526	08646 **F**	08651 **D**	08664	08709	08904
08924 **D**	08944 **D**	08947	09006 **ML**	09007 **ML**	09012 **D**	09016 **D**
09018 **ML**	09020	09101 **D**	09102 **D**			

EWRB   Stratford Class 37/Eastleigh Class 73 (Restricted Use)

37040 **E**	37174 **E**	37194 **FM**	37220 **E**	37245 **C**	37293 **ML**	37370 **E**
37372 **ML**	37380 **FM**	73128 **E**	73131 **E**	73132 **IO**	73139 **IO**	73140 **IO**
73141 **IO**						

EWSF   Stratford Class 08/09

08541 **D**	08593 **O**	08711 **RX**	08750	08752 **C**	08775	08866
08909	09010 **D**					

EWSU   Selhurst Class 08/09

08698   09023

EWSX   Stored/Reserve Shunters

08414 **O**	08460 **O**	08517	08670	08689 **O**	08700	08715 **O**
08740 **F**	08758	08811	08878	08958		

EWS (FORMERLY LOADHAUL)

FDAI   Immingham Class 60

60002 E	60003 E	60004 E	60007 LH	60008 LH	60020 E	60021 F
60023 E	60024 E	60025 LH	60026 E	60027 E	60028 E	60030 E
60031 FS	60038 LH	60049 E	60050 E	60051 E	60052 E	60053 E
60054 FP	60059 LH	60064 FL	60067 F	60068 F	60069 F	60070 FL
60082 FA	60090 FC	60091 FC				

FDBI   Immingham Class 56

56003 LH	56004	56006 LH	56007 FT	56011 F	56021 LH	56022 FT
56025 FT	56027 LH	56029 F	56031 C	56033 FT	56034 LH	56035 LH
56036 CT	56038 FT	56039 LH	56041 E	56043 FS	56045 LH	56046 C
56047 CT	56048 C	56049 CT	56051 E	56054 FT	56055 LH	56059 E
56062 F	56063 F	56065 E	56066 FT	56067 E	56068 U	56069 FS
56070 FT	56071 FT	56074 LH	56075 F	56077 LH	56078 F	56080 F
56081 F	56082 F	56083 LH	56084 LH	56085 LH	56086 FT	56087 E
56088 E	56089 E	56090 LH	56091 F	56092 FT	56093 FT	56094 FC
56095 F	56096 E	56097 FS	56098 F	56099 FT	56100 FT	56101 FT
56102 LH	56105 E	56106 LH	56107 LH	56108 F	56109 LH	56110 LH
56111 LH	56112 LH	56114 E	56116 E	56117 E	56118 LH	56120 E
56125 FT	56126 FC	56127 FT	56130 LH	56131 F	56132 FT	56133 FT
56134 FC	56135 F					

FDCI   Immingham Class 37

37503 E	37513 LH	37515 FS	37516 LH	37517 E	37519 FS	37677 F
37680 FA	37682 E	37684 E	37686 FA	37688 E	37689 F	37694 E
37697 E	37698 LH	37706 E	37707 E	37708 FP	37710 LH	37713 LH
37716 E	37717 E	37718 E	37719 FP	37883 E	37884 LH	37885 E
37886 E						

FDKI   Immingham Class 47 (Control Contingency)

47315 C	47331 C	47476 R	47543 R	47972 CS

FDRI   Immingham Class 37 (Restricted Use)

37131 F	37225 F	37332 FC	37350 FP

FDSD   Doncaster Class 08

08418 F	08500 0	08509 F	08510	08511	08512 F	08514
08587	08877 D					

FDSI   Immingham Class 08

08401 D	08405 D	08632	08665	08824 F	08888 E

FDSK   Knottingley Class 08/09

08442 F	08499 F	08597	08605	08662	08706	08776 D
08782	08783	09014 D				

FDSX   Stored Shunters

08388 **FP**   08445   08466 **FO**   08581 **BS**   08713   08931

FDYX   Stored Locomotives

37003 **C**	37019 **FD**	37058 **C**	37059 **FD**	37063 **FD**	37068 **FD**	37075 **F**
37083 **C**	37101 **FD**	37104 **C**	37110 **F**	37139 **FC**	37144 **FA**	37209 **BR**
37217	37218 **F**	37223 **FC**	37235 **F**	37298 **F**	37330 **BR**	37331 **F**
37335 **F**	37340 **FD**	37341 **F**	37343 **C**	37344 **FD**	37358 **F**	37359 **FP**
37381 **FD**	37382 **FP**	47221 **FP**	47224 **FP**	47256 **FD**	47277 **FD**	47294 **FD**
47319 **FP**	47346 **C**	47352 **C**	47359 **FD**	47369 **FD**	47522 **R**	47550 **M**
47574 **R**	47676 **I**	47677 **I**	56008	56012 **FC**	56014 **FC**	56061 **FS**

FMSY   Thornaby Class 08/09

08577   08582 **D**   08806 **F**   08813 **D**   09005 **D**   09106 **D**   09204 **D**

EUROSTAR (UK)

GPSN   Stewarts Lane Class 73 (North Pole)

73118 **EP**   73130 **EP**

GPSS   Old Oak Common Class 08 (North Pole)

08948 **EP**

GPSV   Old Oak Common Class 37/6

37601 **EP**   37602 **EP**   37603 **EP**   37604 **EP**   37605 **EP**   37606 **EP**

TRAIN OPERATING COMPANIES

HASS   ScotRail Railways – Inverness Class 08

08754   08762

HBSH   Great North Eastern Railway – Bounds Green/Craigentinny Class 08

08331 **GN**   08472   08571   08724   08834 **FD**   08853   08892 **GN**

HEBD   Merseyrail Electrics – Birkenhead North Class 73/0

73002 **BR**   73005   73901 **MD**   73906 **MD**

HFSL   Virgin West Coast – Longsight Class 08

08611   08721 **O**   08790

HFSN   Virgin West Coast – Willesden Class 08

08451   08454   08617   08696 **D**   08887   08934

HGSS   Central Trains – Tyseley Class 08

08616 **G**   08805 **O**

HISE Midland Mainline – Derby Etches Park Class 08

| 08536 | 08690 | 08697 | 08899 |

HISL Midland Mainline – Neville Hill Class 08

| 08525 F | 08588 BS | 08908 | 08950 I |

HJSE Great Western Trains – Landore Class 08

| 08780 | 08795 M | 08822 M |

HJSL Great Western Trains – Laira Class 08

| 08641 D | 08644 M | 08645 D | 08648 D | 08663 D |

HJXX Great Western Trains – Old Oak Common/St Phillips Marsh Class 08

| 08410 D | 08483 D | 08643 D | 08836 I |

HLSV Cardiff Railway Co. – Cardiff Canton Class 08

| 08830 G |

HSSN Anglia Railways – Norwich Crown Point Class 08

| 08810 | 08869 G | 08928 FR |

HWSU Connex South Central – Selhurst Class 09

| 09004 | 09025 | 09026 D |

HYSB South Western Trains – Bournemouth Class 73/1

| 73109 SC |

INTERCITY TRAIN OPERATING UNITS

IANA Anglia Railways – Norwich Crown Point Class 86/2

| 86215 I | 86217 I | 86218 I | 86220 I | 86221 I | 86223 I | 86230 I |
| 86232 I | 86235 I | 86237 I | 86238 I | 86246 I | 86250 I | 86257 I |

ICCA Virgin Cross Country – Longsight Class 86/2

86204 I	86205 I	86206 I	86212 I	86213 I	86214 I	86222 I
86226 I	86227 I	86229 I	86233 I	86234 I	86244 I	86247 I
86252 I	86255 I	86259 I	86260 I			

ICCP Virgin Cross Country – Neville Hill/Laira Class 43

43087 I	43088 I	43089 I	43090 I	43091 I	43101 I	43102 I
43103 I	43121 I	43122 I	43153 V	43154 I	43155 V	43156 I
43157 I	43158 I	43159 I	43160 I	43161 I	43162 I	43193 I
43194 I	43195 I	43196 I	43197 I	43198 I		

ICCS Virgin Cross Country – Edinburgh Craigentinny Class 43

43013 I	43014 I	43062 I	43063 V	43065 I	43067 I	43068 V
43069 I	43070 I	43071 I	43078 I	43079 I	43080 I	43084 I
43086 I	43092 V	43093 V	43094 I	43097 I	43098 I	43099 I
43100 I	43123 I					

IECA   Great North Eastern Railway – Bounds Green Class 91

91001 **GN**	91002 **GN**	91003 **GN**	91004 **GN**	91005 **GN**	91006 **GN**	91007 **GN**
91008 **GN**	91009 **GN**	91010 **GN**	91011 **GN**	91012 **GN**	91013 **GN**	91014 **GN**
91015 **GN**	91016 **GN**	91017 **GN**	91018 **GN**	91019 **GN**	91020 **GN**	91021 **GN**
91022 **GN**	91023 **GN**	91024 **GN**	91025 **GN**	91026 **GN**	91027 **GN**	91028 **GN**
91029 **GN**	91030 **GN**	91031 **GN**				

IECB   Great North Eastern Railway – Bounds Green Class 89

89001 **GN**

IECP   Great North Eastern Railway – Craigentinny/Neville Hill Class 43

43038 **GN**	43039 **GN**	43095 **GN**	43096 **GN**	43105 **GN**	43106 **GN**	43107 **GN**
43108 **GN**	43109 **GN**	43110 **GN**	43111 **GN**	43112 **GN**	43113 **GN**	43114 **GN**
43115 **GN**	43116 **GN**	43117 **GN**	43118 **GN**	43119 **GN**	43120 **GN**	43167 **GN**

ILRA   Virgin Cross Country – Bristol Bath Road Class 47/8

47805 **I**	47806 **I**	47807 **PL**	47810 **I**	47812 **I**	47814 **V**	47817 **PL**
47818 **I**	47822 **I**	47825 **I**	47826 **I**	47827 **I**	47828 **I**	47829 **I**
47831 **I**	47839 **I**	47840 **I**	47841 **I**	47843 **I**	47844 **V**	47847 **I**
47848 **I**	47849 **I**	47851 **I**	47853 **I**	47854 **I**		

IMLP   Midland Mainline – Neville Hill Class 43

43043 **MM**	43044 **I**	43045 **I**	43046 **I**	43047 **I**	43048 **I**	43049 **MM**
43050 **I**	43051 **I**	43052 **I**	43053 **I**	43054 **I**	43055 **I**	43056 **I**
43057 **I**	43058 **MM**	43059 **MM**	43060 **I**	43061 **I**	43064 **I**	43066 **MM**
43072 **I**	43073 **I**	43074 **MM**	43075 **I**	43076 **MM**	43077 **MM**	43081 **I**
43082 **I**	43083 **I**	43085 **I**	43180 **I**			

IVGA   Gatwick Express – Stewarts Lane Class 73

73201 **GX**	73202 **GX**	73203 **GX**	73204 **GX**	73205 **GX**	73206 **GX**	73207 **GX**
73208 **GX**	73209 **GX**	73210 **GX**	73211 **GX**	73212 **GX**	73213 **GX**	73235 **GX**

IWCA   Virgin West Coast – Willesden Class 87/90

87001 **I**	87002 **I**	87003 **I**	87004 **I**	87005 **I**	87006 **I**	87007 **I**
87008 **I**	87009 **I**	87010 **I**	87011 **I**	87012 **I**	87013 **I**	87014 **I**
87015 **I**	87016 **I**	87017 **I**	87018 **I**	87019 **I**	87020 **I**	87021 **I**
87022 **I**	87023 **I**	87024 **I**	87025 **I**	87026 **I**	87027 **I**	87028 **I**
87029 **I**	87030 **I**	87031 **I**	87032 **I**	87033 **I**	87034 **I**	87035 **I**
90001 **I**	90002 **V**	90003 **I**	90004 **I**	90005 **I**	90006 **I**	90007 **I**
90008 **I**	90009 **I**	90010 **I**	90011 **I**	90012 **I**	90013 **I**	90014 **V**
90015 **V**						

IWCP   Virgin West Coast – Manchester Longsight Class 43

43028 **I**	43029 **I**	43041 **I**	43042 **I**	43164 **I**	43165 **I**	43166 **I**

IWLA   Great Western Trains – Laira Class 47

47815 **I**	47816 **I**	47832 **I**	47846 **U**

IWLX   Great Western Trains – Laira Class 47 (Reserve)

47811 **I**	47813 **I**	47845 **I**

IWPA   Virgin West Coast – Willesden Class 86

86102 I	86207 I	86209 I	86224 I	86225 I	86231 I	86236 I
86240 I	86242 I	86245 I	86248 I	86251 I	86253 I	86256 I
86258 I						

IWRP   Great Western Trains – Laira/St Phillips Marsh Class 43

43002 I	43003 GW	43004 GW	43005 GW	43006 I	43007 I	43008 GW
43009 I	43010 GW	43011 GW	43012 GW	43015 GW	43016 I	43017 I
43018 GW	43019 I	43020 GW	43021 I	43022 I	43023 I	43024 I
43025 I	43026 GW	43027 I	43030 GW	43031 I	43032 GW	43033 I
43034 I	43035 I	43036 I	43037 I	43040 I	43124 GW	43125 I
43126 I	43127 I	43128 I	43129 GW	43130 I	43131 GW	43132 GW
43133 I	43134 I	43135 GW	43136 GW	43137 GW	43138 GW	43139 GW
43140 GW	43141 GW	43142 GW	43143 I	43144 I	43145 I	43146 I
43147 I	43148 I	43149 I	43150 I	43151 I	43152 I	43163 I
43168 GW	43169 I	43170 GW	43171 I	43172 I	43173 I	43174 GW
43175 I	43176 I	43177 GW	43178 I	43179 GW	43181 I	43182 GW
43183 GW	43184 I	43185 GW	43186 GW	43187 GW	43188 GW	43189 GW
43190 GW	43191 GW	43192 GW				

EWS (FORMERLY TRANSRAIL)

LBBS   Bescot Class 08

08542 F	08543 D	08601 0	08623	08628	08746 D	08765 D
08807 BS	08920 F	08927	09104 D			

LBSB   Bescot Class 37 (Sandite Fitted)

37012 C	37154 FT	37196 C	37255 C	37258 C

LCWX   Strategic Reserve Locomotives

08428	08519 0	08622	08693	08731	08734	08815
08826	08938 0	08952	20118 FR	20132 FR	20138 FR	20165 FR
20168	20169 CS	31106 C	31107 C	31119 C	31126 C	31130 FC
31132 FO	31134 C	31144 C	31147 C	31164 FO	31178 C	31185 C
31190 C	31199 FC	31206 C	31224 C	31232 C	31235 C	31237 C
31238 C	31242 C	31270 FC	31275 FC	31285 C	31302 FP	31317 FO
31319 FC	31327 FR	31405 M	31410 RR	31514 C	31421 RR	31422 M
31423 M	31524 C	31427	31530 C	31432	31435 C	31537 C
31538	31545	31546 C	31455 RR	31556 C	31462 D	31468 C
37026 FD	37045 F	37087 C	37088 CT	37107 FD	37108 F	37111 FT
37142 C	37156 FT	37178 F	37184 C	37188 C	37201 CT	37207 C
37213 FC	37214 FT	37232 CT	37240 C	37251 I	37334 F	37904 FS
37905 FS	37906 FT	47193 FP	47295 FP	47300 C	47308 C	47329 C
47332 C	47333 C	47334 C	47341 C	47353 C	47372 C	47478
47513 BR	47524 RX	47530 RX	47532 RX	47536 RX	47566 RX	47576 RX
47628 RX	47704 RX	47715 N	47716 RX	56019 FR	56060 FT	

LCXX   Stored Locomotives

08448	08586 F	08610	08619	08625	08683	08718
08893 D	08901	08911 D	08914	20016	20057	20059 FR
20066	20081	20087 BS	20092 CS	31102 C	31125 C	31128 FO
31145 C	31155 FA	31158 C	31160 F	31171 FO	31174 C	31200 FC
31248 FO	31263 C	31301 FR	31304 FC	31312 FC	31408	31411 D
31415	31516 C	31417 D	31519 C	31526 C	31533 C	31444 C
31548 C	37078 FS	47238 FD	47357 C			

LGAM   Motherwell Class 56

56050 LH	56056 FT	56057 E	56058 E	56072 FT	56079 FT	56104 FC
56123 FT	56124 FC	56128 FT	56129 FT			

LGBM   Motherwell Class 37

37043 CT	37069 C	37100 FT	37152 I	37153 CT	37165 C	37170 C
37175 C	37221 FT	37250 FT	37261 FD	37294 C	37351 CT	37510 I
37675 FT	37683 FT	37685 I	37692 FC	37693 FT	37702 FT	37712 E
37714 E	37796 FC	37797 FC	37799 FT	37801 E	37802 FT	37893 E

LGHM   Motherwell Class 37/4 (West Highland)

37401 FT	37403 G	37404 FT	37406 FT	37409 FT	37410 FT	37413 FT
37424 FT	37428 F	37430 FT				

LGML   Motherwell Class 08/09

08411	08506	08534 D	08561	08630	08675 F	08685
08720 D	08735	08738 D	08768	08827	08881 D	08882
08883 O	08906	08910	08912 BS	08922 D	09103 D	09202 D
09205 D						

LNAK   Cardiff Canton Class 60

60009 E	60012 E	60015 FT	60016 E	60017 E	60034 FT	60035 FT
60037 E	60041 E	60062 FT	60063 FT	60080 FT	60081 FT	60084 FT
60089 FT	60093 FT	60096 FT				

LNBK   Cardiff Canton Class 56

56010 FT	56018 FT	56032 E	56037 E	56040 FT	56044 FT	56052 FT
56053 FT	56064 FT	56073 FT	56076 FS	56103 E	56113 FT	56115 FT
56119 FT	56121 FC					

LNCF   Cardiff Canton Class 08/09/97

08481	08493	08576	08756 D	08770 D	08786 D	08792
08798	08801	08819 D	08828 E	08941	08953 D	08957 E
09001	09008 D	09013 D	09015 D	09105 D	09107 D	09203 D

LNCK   Cardiff Canton Class 37 (Wales)

37411 E	37412 FT	37416 E	37427 E	37701 FT	37704 E	37887 FT
37888 F	37889 FT	37894 FC	37895 E	37896 FT	37897 FT	37898 FT
37899 E	37901 FT	37902 FS	37903 FS			

LNLK Cardiff Canton Class 37 (St Blazey)

37521 E	37668 E	37669 E	37670 FT	37671 FT	37672 FD	37673 FT
37674 FT	37696 FT					

LNSK Cardiff Canton Class 37 (Sandite Fitted)

37197 CT	37229 FC	37230 CT	37254 C	37263 C	37275

LNWK Cardiff Canton Class 08 (Allied Steel & Wire)

08900 D	08932	08942	08954 FT	08955	08993 FT	08994 D
08995 FT						

LWCW Crewe Diesel Class 37/47 (Freight)

37025 BR	37073 FT	37095 C	37116 0	37141 C	37146 C	37158 C
37191 C	37211 C	37212 FT	37402 F	37407 FT	37408 BR	37417 F
37505 FT	37509 F	37518 E	37520 E	37667 E	37678 F	37695 E
47016 FO	47475 RX	47520 I	47523 M	47528 M	47535 RX	47711 N

LWMC Crewe Diesel Class 37/4 (North West Passenger)

37414 RR	37415 E	37418 E	37419 E	37420 RR	37421 E	37422 RR
37425 RR	37426 E	37429 RR				

LWNW Crewe Diesel Class 31

31110 C	31113 C	31142 C	31146 C	31154 C	31163 C	31166 C
31188 C	31201 FC	31203 C	31207 C	31229 C	31233 C	31255 C
31273 C	31306 C	31308 C	31407 ML	31420 M	31434	
31439 RR	31450	31554 C	31465 RR	31466 C	31467	

LWSP Crewe Diesel Class 08

08397 F	08402 D	08485	08489 F	08676	08695	08817 BS
08867 0	08884	08894	08915 F	08918 D	08925	

HERITAGE LOCOMOTIVES

MBDL Diesel Locomotives

46035 G   55022 G

MBEL Electric Locomotives

71001 G

EWS (FORMERLY RES)

PXLB   Crewe Diesel Class 47 (Extended Range)

47721 **RX**	47722 **RX**	47725 **RX**	47726 **RX**	47727 **RX**	47732 **RX**	47733 **RX**
47734 **RX**	47736 **RX**	47737 **RX**	47738 **RX**	47739 **RX**	47741 **RX**	47742 **RX**
47744 **RX**	47745 **RX**	47746 **RX**	47747 **RX**	47749 **RX**	47750 **RX**	47756 **RX**
47757 **RX**	47758 **RX**	47759 **RX**	47760 **RX**	47761 **RX**	47762 **RX**	47763 **RX**
47764 **RX**	47765 **RX**	47766 **RX**	47767 **RX**	47768 **RX**	47769 **RX**	47770 **RX**
47771 **RX**	47772 **RX**	47773 **RX**	47774 **RX**	47775 **RX**	47776 **RX**	47777 **RX**
47778 **RX**	47779 **RX**	47780 **RX**	47781 **RX**	47782 **RX**	47783 **RX**	47784 **RX**
47785 **E**	47786 **E**	47787 **RX**	47788 **RX**	47789 **RX**	47790 **RX**	47791 **RX**
47792 **RX**	47793 **RX**					

PXLC   Crewe Diesel Class 47

47467 **BR**	47492 **RX**	47501 **R**	47565 **RX**	47572 **R**	47575 **R**	47584 **RX**
47596 **RX**	47624 **RX**	47627 **RX**	47634 **R**	47635 **R**	47640 **R**	

PXLE   Crewe Electric Class 86/90

86208 **I**	86210 **RX**	86241 **RX**	86243 **RX**	86254 **RX**	86261 **E**	86401 **RX**
86416 **RX**	86417 **RX**	86419 **RX**	86424 **RX**	86425 **RX**	86426 **E**	86430 **RX**
90016 **RX**	90017 **RX**	90018 **RX**	90019 **RX**	90020 **E**		

PXLK   Crewe Diesel Class 47/9

47971 **BR**   47976 **C**

PXLP   Crewe Diesel Class 47 (VIP Fleet)

47798 **0**   47799 **0**

PXLS   Crewe Diesel/Heaton/Willesden Class 08

08578 **R**	08633 **RX**	08635	08701 **RX**	08702	08742 **RX**	08757 **RX**
08802 **RX**	08804	08873 **RX**	08890 **D**	08896	08897 **D**	08919 **RX**
08921 **E**						

PXXA   Stored Locomotives

08594	08599	47471 **I0**	47474 **R**	47481 **BR**	47489 **R**	47539 **RX**
47547 **N**	47717 **R**				

EVERSHOLT HOLDINGS

SAXL   Locomotives Off Lease

86101 **I**   86103 **I**   86216 **I**   86219 **I**   86228 **I**   86249 **I**

PORTERBROOK LEASING COMPANY

SBXL   Locomotives Off Lease

47830 **I**

ANGEL TRAIN CONTRACTS

SCXL   **Locomotives Off Lease**
43104 I

OTHER OPERATORS

XHSD   **Direct Rail Services Class 20/3**
20301 **0**   20302 **0**   20303 **0**   20304 **0**   20305 **0**

XYPA   **ARC Class 59/1**
59101 **0**   59102 **0**   59103 **0**   59104 **0**

XYPD   **Hunslet Barclay Class 20/9**
20901 **0**   20902 **0**   20903 **0**   20904 **0**   20905 **0**   20906 **0**

XYPN   **National Power Class 59/2**
59201 **0**   59202 **0**   59203 **0**   59204 **0**   59205 **0**   59206 **0**

XYPO   **Foster Yeoman Class 59/0**
59001 **0**   59002 **0**   59004 **0**   59005 **0**

LIVERY CODES

Locomotives are BR blue unless otherwise indicated. The colour of the lower half of the bodyside is stated first. Minor variations to these liveries are ignored.

BR Revised BR blue (blue with yellow cabs, grey roof, large numbers and full height BR logo).

BS BR blue with red solebar stripe.

C Civil Engineers (grey and yellow with black cab doors and window surrounds).

CS Central services (grey and red).

CT Civil Engineers livery with Transrail lettering and markings (large white 'T' on a blue circle with a red outline underlined with red stripes).

D Departmental (plain grey with black cab doors and window surrounds).

E English, Welsh & Scottish Railway (maroon with large maroon EW&S or EWS lettering and number on broad gold band between cabs).

EP Eurostar (UK) locomotive livery (as **F** with blue roof and cast Channel Tunnel logo).

F New Railfreight (two-tone grey with black cab doors and window surrounds).

FA Trainload Construction (as **F** with Trainload Construction markings (blue blocks on a yellow background)).

FC Trainload Coal (as **F** with Trainload Coal markings (black diamonds on a yellow background)).

FD Old Railfreight Distribution (as **F** with Railfreight Distribution markings (red diamonds on a yellow background)).

FE New Railfreight Distribution (two-tone grey with blue roof, black lower bodyside Railfreight Distribution lettering and RfD markings (red diamonds on a yellow background)).

FF Freightliner (as **F** with black Freightliner lettering and red markings (diagonal stripes behind right hand cab door)).

FL New Railfreight Livery with Loadhaul lettering.

FM New Railfreight Livery with Mainline markings.

FO Old Railfreight (grey sides, yellow cabs and full height BR logo).

FP Trainload Petroleum (as **F** with Trainload Petroleum markings (blue waves on a yellow background)).

FR Old Railfreight Revised (as **FO** but with a red solebar stripe and a slightly smaller BR logo).

FS Trainload Metals (as **F** with Trainload Metals markings (blue chevrons on a yellow background)).

FT New Railfreight Livery with Transrail lettering and markings (large white 'T' on a blue circle with a red outline underlined with red stripes).

G BR or GWR green.

GE Gatwick Express (white and dark grey with claret stripe and Gatwick Express lettering and motif).

GN Great North Eastern Railway (dark blue with an orange bodyside stripe and gold or silver GNER lettering).

GW Great Western Trains (green and ivory with Great Western Trains logo and lettering).

I InterCity (white and dark grey with red stripe and swallow motif).

IO Old InterCity (light grey and dark grey with red stripe, yellow lower cab sides and BR logo).

LH Loadhaul (black with orange cabsides and Loadhaul lettering).

M Mainline (as **IO** but without the yellow lower cabsides and BR logo).

MD Merseyrail Departmental (dark grey and yellow with Merseyrail logo and lettering).

ML Mainline Freight (blue with silver body stripe and Mainline logo and lettering).

MM Midland Mainline (grey and green with three orange bodyside stripes and Midland Mainline logo and lettering).

N Network SouthEast (grey/white/red/white/blue/white).

O Other livery (non-standard - refer to text).

PL Porterbrook Leasing (purple at one end, white at the other with small logo and lettering behind the left-hand cab doors. The livery represents an enlarged portion of the Porterbrook logo with the colours reversed on the other side).

R Parcels (post office red and dark grey).

RR Regional Railways (grey/light blue/white/dark blue).

RX Rail express systems (post office red with Res blue & black markings)

SC Stagecoach (grey/orange/red/white/blue/white).

T Racal-BRT (two-tone grey with green markings).

U Grey undercoat. (certain locos emerged in undercoat whilst EWS and Great Western Trains were deciding on a livery to adopt as standard).

V Virgin Trains (red with black cabs extending into bodysides, three white lower bodysides stripes and small Virgin logo behind cab doors on locos or red with black inner ends and large full height Virgin logo on Class 43 power cars).

W Waterman Railways (black with cream & red lining).
